Mythical Lovers,
Divine Desires

'To desire and to see through desire –
this is the courage that the heart requires.'

James Hillman, 'Thought of the Heart'

Mythical Lovers, Divine Desires

THE WORLD'S GREAT LOVE LEGENDS

Sarah Bartlett

BLANDFORD

A BLANDFORD BOOK

First published in the UK 1988 by Blandford
a Cassell imprint

Cassell plc
Wellington House
125 Strand
London WC2R 0BB

Distributed in the United States by Sterling Publishing Co., Inc.
387 Park Avenue South, New York, NY 10016-8810

A Cataloguing-in-Publication Data entry for this title is available
from the British Library

ISBN 0-7137-2718-7

Designed by Chris Bell
Printed and bound in Great Britain by The Bath Press, Bath

Contents

Preface

HIS book brings together some of the world's most evocative myths about lovers and divine desire to reveal the extraordinary parity of human experience across civilizations and cultures that are separated by both time and geographical space.

The search for a meaning in life has been manifested in many forms throughout the history of mankind. Spiritual practice, sacred sexuality, ritual and religion have evolved over thousands of years to align with different cultural values and needs. But no matter what differences occur, the basic experience of being human remains unchanged.

Once upon a time we were in touch with the earth and with the nature of being. We nurtured ourselves and lived with the rhythms of nature and the balance of the 'whole' rather than just for the 'self'. It seems that our perception of our inner landscape, of this place where we can get in touch with the whole, had to change as our outer landscape became distorted and reshaped out of all recognition with the development of our own consciousness. Attending to our outer landscape means that we forget to keep in touch with our inner one, and our ego's attachment to how it appears outwardly means we lose connection to our soul.

'Soul' is not a sentimental concept. In early Greek religious practice the goddess Psyche personified soul, that inner place we share with every other human being. Soul lives within, and without, and will sometimes call for us when we least expect it. We, who no longer seek to follow the way into the inner landscape, often find soul coming out of the unconscious to snatch at us, to kidnap us and take us there. Whether it is hidden beneath the mask of compelling passion or that seemingly irresistible moment of falling in love, this is the way we come to know soul.

In the West it is often through such relationships, through another human being, that we also search desperately for something, not knowing it is to be found within ourselves. Passion makes us feel alive, makes us sing, makes us feel in touch with something powerful and wonderful, just as it would if we followed this meaning in life in a more spiritual practice. We have been cut off from our souls in the West, and because romantic love has become our religion, we think we can find fulfilment through this extraordinary and powerful force that draws us into an illusion of

Vertumnus, disguised as an old woman, visits Pomona.

permanence. In many other cultures, romantic love, passion and desire are acknowledged as being such, and divine or transpersonal love is found through religious or spiritual journeys.

The powerful imagery of myth has often been a pathway to understanding the mystery of being. These myths are the 'carriers' of our universal affinity to know who we are and our quest for wholeness. Carl Gustav Jung called mythical archetypes 'great dreams of humanity', and he also believed that 'we have recollected ourselves from the Universe' and that our projections happen to us, rather than we 'make them happen'. In a sense, it is the idea that has you, rather than you having the idea; it is the myth dreaming you, rather than you dreaming the myth. We simply act out the dramas of the great play that is being written. The collective unconscious has been at work since the dawn of humankind.

Sex gods, fertility goddesses and mythical lovers, whether in human or animal form, have always been an important symbol and projection of our need to understand who we really are. The power of love, and of transformation within, is reflected through the imagery of passionate gods and goddesses and their myths, of tragic lovers and of eternal compassion. The divine desire and sacred sexuality that connects us to soul, beyond the duality of our perception of life, can be glimpsed by way of love's transformation in mythical guise.

This collection of myths of passion and romance reveals the universal similarity of love. Not only do they raise, again and again, the question 'What is love?' but also the question 'Why is love?' For thousands of years humans have sought to re-connect to their souls, to the very source of life itself, through myths that reflect personal emotions.

This book offers a selection of some of the most evocative tales of mythical lovers and divine desire. Each myth includes a brief introduction to the traditional and cultural setting of the myth or deity concerned. The roots of every culture grow differently, but the essence of 'love' never changes. It is ineffable, intangible, and mostly indestructible. The myths also include reflections on both the psychological and spiritual symbolism – the psychological significance for us as individuals and in terms of the unconscious shadow that lurks collectively; the spiritual, in terms of how love and human sexuality are powerful forces that have been long removed from our ancient connections to nature and the rhythms of life.

Love is a mystery to be lived, and it is through myth that the mystery can become truly alive for each of us.

Introduction

LOVE and lovers, whether in human or animal form, often play an integral part in myths as a projection of our search for 'self'. The tragedy of love affairs, the pain of loss, the separation of 'twin souls' or unrequited love are different aspects of the human need to relate and to find out what this mysterious thing 'love' is all about.

Once we are 'in love', we become enmeshed in our own subjectivity. There is no way out; we can pass only further and further in, either until the image dissolves and we reclaim our love of self or until the pain becomes unbearable, the image is shattered and we turn to another mirror to reflect our soul again. The paradox is that by being 'in love' we are in fact falling in love with ourselves, and we have an opportunity to see ourselves in the eyes of another. It is an ecstatic place to be, the dance of romantic love, and one that cannot be denied, for it is the place where we are most likely to experience a divine tango with our soul. Love and myth go hand in hand, for myth is the most exquisite mirror of all for the reflection of self.

Human sexuality is also about a re-connection to the divine. For thousands of years fertility goddesses and their consorts were sacred aspects of spiritual belief. Long before the patriarchal societies emerged, the goddess played a role that was creative, fertile, productive and

10

essentially nurturing. Sexual union was both sacred and profane, but on the level of the divine, it was a means by which humans could attempt to transcend the mundane world. In many civilizations both philosophy and religion were profoundly connected to sexual practices. Deities and their sexual worship were neither frowned upon nor regarded as anything other than another aspect of the richness of life, which could lead to higher spiritual awareness or transcendence of the illusion of the material world.

Some civilizations see only the outer physical world as real, and reject the idea that there is an inner landscape, a universal unconscious or an energy that connects the whole of the cosmos, both infinitely and eternally. Others believe only in the inner world, and the transcendence of form, boundaries and physical illusion. But both are true. It is only when we try to find the inner world solely through our outer relationships that we create a false reality.

What is love?

This question can only be answered by each of us individually, for everyone perceives love in a different way, depending on our degree of level of awareness and on our environment and our social and cultural backgrounds. In the West, however, it seems that we generally confuse three different kinds of love – personal, interpersonal and transpersonal – and 'download' them into one other person with high expectations that all-round fulfilment will thereby be found.

The ancient Greeks had many different words for love, including *epithemia*, *philia*, *eros* and *agape*. I have defined these four here to illustrate how love evolves and changes and is unrestricted beneath the layers of language we have created to give it form.

The ancient Greeks believed *epithemia* to be the natural, instinctual urge we all have to touch and to be touched and caressed. *Epithemia* is concerned with pleasure for self and the body's need to be physically aroused and nurtured. It is about sensual love and the pleasuring of oneself. The word was used to describe the body's unconscious need for sensuality and basic sexual release. There were no romantic or erotic connotations to this animal drive and desire; it was neither judged nor was it considered immoral. It was only the teachings of Judaeo-Christianity that condemned such basic sexual desire as perverse and subsequently urged society to sublimate such instincts.

Philia was a love that could exist without any sense of *epithemia*. *Philia* was about idealization, like the first stirrings of romantic desire. It is similar to adolescent worship and the idolization of another human being, whether of the same sex or not. When we first fall in love, when we first see the other person as someone quite separate from ourselves, it also allows us to feel good about who we are. Wooing and courtship are aspects of *philia* but without sexual involvement. It is the ability to see the other person as separate from ourselves, but at the same time also awakening our own inner qualities. When we do this we are inspired and gradually begin to see ourselves and others as different. However, we still idolize and idealize the other, put him or her on a pedestal and believe he

Zeus and Danae

12

or she can do no wrong. The 'other' becomes an idealized vision of our own inner heart. And this is where *philia* often loses touch with its own model, and seeks out *eros*.

Erotic love is one on which we in the West have become most hooked. When Christianity merged with the ideals of courtly love, medieval romance was seen as the purist form of *philia*, and *epithemia* was forced underground. Erotic love subsequently undermined romantic passion and the divine ecstasy of spiritual love, to bind them inextricably together in the Western psyche. Now we can think of love only as a merger of romance and erotic passion. It is as if *eros* has become the most troublesome trigger for our hearts and our souls.

Eros is more than simply our modern association with the word erotic, however. For the Greeks, erotic love was about transformation, about the desire to unite, rather than simply the pleasure of physical ecstasy. But merging souls and psyches often leads to pain, especially when we link *epithemia* and *eros* with high expectations. Erotic love involves some element of pain and suffering because in any transformation something is lost. Those moments of ecstasy, whether sexual or simply intellectual passion, cannot last forever. Once we have experienced such intensity, the separation can be unbearably painful. But falling into the well of erotic love means we also have to honour the fact that the deeper we fall down the hole, the more painful the landing.

Eros was once evoked through group rituals, such as the Roman Saturnalia or the Greek Bacchanalia. The Greeks also found ways to channel their erotic feelings through drama and plays. The audience could thus identify with an archetype, rather than allowing such overwhelming energy to surge up from their unconscious.

Pouring passion into a one-to-one relationship means we have huge expectations and ideals about how that relationship is going to carry *eros* for us permanently, but it usually cannot, for *eros* is about mystery, and how can mystery be sustained when you have grown to know someone intimately and well?

Agape means 'the love of god for man'. It was not necessarily a non-sexual word, because the Greek gods were notorious for having sexual relations with mortals. But this kind of love was non-attached, sexual loving. Again the Christians distorted this kind of love so that it became entirely sexless. Celibacy was part of divine love, and godliness became 'sexlessness' to the Christians. To the ancient Greeks, godliness was sexiness. *Agape* is very different from *eros*, *epithemia* and *philia* in that it is not possessive. It is detached love; it allows the other to be free, and it allows the other room to be him- or herself. It can involve sexual relationship, but it also involves a powerful spiritual sense of loving; the difference being that it is non-binding and unconditional.

Our expectations of finding happiness, of finding *epithemia*, *philia*, *eros* and possibly *agape* all in one other human being, has put impossible demands on us all.

The Mystery of Love and Desire

If we remembered the past, the past of all our ancestors, and the past they carried with them from the long past, perhaps we would remember that love is not so much about desire but about human compassion and a reconnection to soul. However, it is desire that is often the very thing that leads us to the place where we could find our soul, into the realms of the unconscious. This is the paradox of desire.

The word desire is rooted in the Latin, *de sidera*, which means 'the absence of stars'. When the night was dark there would be no stars to be guided by; if you have nothing to guide you, you are lost. You may find yourself in unknown territory, you may be led only by instinct, compelled by something unknown, rather than by looking at the map, by knowing the truth of the stars. In this sense, the stars represent consciousness, the ability to look at a system, a scheme, and to know our way or direction. The 'absence of stars', or 'desire', leads us only into unconscious realms. If we are looking for a star and miss sight of it, then we are lost.

Following our desires is to navigate with no stars. Yet the irony is that by following desire, we are offered the opportunity to meet with 'soul' and thereby perhaps at least begin to take a few steps towards the journey within. For although the inner landscape can never be made conscious, it is from this very place that the soul comes tentatively forth. Desire is like

14

being out of control – there are no stars to steer by – and the archetypal forces surge out of our unconscious and take over our lives in the form of passion, frenzied sexual desire or erotic love. They have come to tell us what we have yet to learn about ourselves.

The paradox of desire is that it moves us – it possesses us, not we it. It comes to us to make us feel whole and, at moments, complete. Passionate love is a mystery. It is like being overwhelmed by something bigger than ourselves, and it is as transcendental as any enlightening experience. If we take the moment and treasure it and know it for what it really is, perhaps we can begin to have more compassion – as well as passion – for those who stir that very desire within our soul.

Tristan and Iseult

Origins and Traditions

THIS is, without doubt, one of the best known myths of romantic frustration and doomed love, and over the years poets and writers have adapted and blended different versions of the essential ingredients of this tragic tale. The earliest recorded version is believed to be that of a poet called Béroul, who was writing in French in the middle of the twelfth century. Although it is often regarded as an Irish Celtic legend, it seems likely that its origins lie in Brittany, from where it eventually became attached to the Arthurian stories of England.

As a myth it shines out from many others that deal with the passions of courtly love and romantic desire. Its painful account of betrayal and self-destruction when passionate love becomes too unbearable a test in life is a familiar theme in subsequent Western literature.

The great French scholar Charles Joseph Bédier (1864-1938) discovered that all the versions of the Tristan stories seem to originate from one myth. Scholars believe that there was one single poem, now lost, from which all the others were adapted. Béroul's version encompasses all the archetypal elements, which merge to produce this vivid tale of passion. It is from both Bédier's magical, beautiful and inspiring retelling of the tale and the translation of Béroul's original work that I have tried to re-create the essence of the myth.

The spirit of the plot, the magic potion, is what drives this myth into its realm of a surprisingly dark psychological and spiritual analogy. Robert A. Johnson has written probably one of the most illuminating works on the Jungian symbolism and psychology of Tristan and Iseult, and I have referred to this where necessary in the reflections section, along with some thoughts of my own.

The Myth

BLANCHEFLEUR, the great queen of Lyonesse, lay dying, and yet her child had only just been born. As she held the tiny infant to her milk-white breast she had time only to name him before her life flew from her. 'You shall be Tristan, the child of sadness, for only in sadness have you known me.'

So Tristan was orphaned. His father, King Rivalen, had been killed by tyrants in France, and so he grew up under the protection of Lord Roholt, the king's loyal marshal, believing that Roholt was his true father. As he grew older he learned the arts of barony and of knighthood, and he was the best huntsman and the proudest and bravest swordsman. All who knew him believed him to be Roholt's son, but Roholt knew him to be the king's son and, by right, his own king.

Tristan travelled widely, and eventually Roholt felt it was time that he should visit Tintagel, so that he could be acknowledged by King Mark, even though he was unaware of his royal connection. King Mark of Cornwall was Blanchefleur's brother, and when he saw Tristan standing before him, a sudden glimmer of his sister's memory poured into his heart. At that moment, Mark had a flash of awareness of Tristan's real identity: his sister's child. With great tenderness he cared for Tristan, and allowed him to stay a while and play his lyre to the court.

'You play and sing well, Tristan. We hope that you may stay a long time with us, friend.'

'I would stay here and serve you faithfully and for as long as you desire, my lord,' replied Tristan.

So the king became like a father to Tristan. Their friendship developed and their love grew like a bond between them.

For three years Tristan lived happily at King Mark's court, and then one day the loyal marshal, Roholt, came to Cornwall to visit Tristan and make sure that he was safe. Now it was time for Tristan to learn of his true parentage, and when he realized that he was heir to the throne of Lyonesse and the nephew of King Mark, he returned to France to fight the tyrants across the sea. When he had defeated the cruel enemy, he asked that Roholt rule the kingdom in his stead, for his only wish was to serve his lord, Mark of Cornwall.

King Mark was dealing with the giant Morholt, the brother of the sorceress queen of Ireland, who had come with his band of raiders to collect tribute from Cornwall. For many years there had been constant war between Ireland and Cornwall. Ireland was a great kingdom, and every fourth year the Cornish people were angered and enraged at the demands of the Irish king. The Cornish people were to send as tribute 300 youths and 300 maidens to be slaves in Ireland, but King Mark had refused to pay these demands and now the mighty Morholt had landed in Cornwall again. He stood at court, offering a trial by combat as the only way out for the Cornish barons and knights. But no one dared fight him, knowing him to be the most powerful warrior in Ireland. Then Tristan stood before the court. Kneeling before the king, he asked: 'My liege, allow me to do battle with the mighty Morholt, for I alone can save you from this tribute.'

Sadly the king nodded his head in assent, and Tristan and Morholt were sent away to a tiny island to fight to the death. For three days the Cornish people gathered on the rocky shores and gazed across to the island, unsure if Tristan would return alive. The women mourned and performed their rituals, preparing their hearts for sadness in case Tristan died. Then, on the third evening, as the golden sun was setting below the horizon, they saw Morholt's boat drifting towards them, its sail billowing gold in the gentle breeze that had lifted across the sea. In their despair they cried, certain now that Tristan had been killed. But as the boat came closer, they saw Tristan standing on the bow, two swords gleaming in the fading sunlight. The good knight pulled the boat up on the shore, and Morholt's men turned their heads to the sand and wept.

'Morholt fought, but not as well as I, my lords. This sword has lost a piece of steel, and it is that steel that still lies embedded in Morholt's head. Go to the island and find his body there, and you will know that it is I who killed him. This is your tribute, sirs!'

But on his return to the castle at Tintagel, amid the cheers from the crowds and the garlands of flowers that lay around his feet, Tristan collapsed in the arms of the king. His wounds were more grievous than any had dared imagine, and they would not heal. Tristan's life blood began to drain away. There were only two people who knew the secret potion that could heal such afflictions, and they were the sorceress queen of Ireland and her daughter, Iseult.

Iseult and her mother had set Morholt's body on a golden altar. Each day they mourned and tended the body ready for burial, and each day they became more bitter and cursed the name of Tristan of Lyonesse. As anger grew in their hearts, so did their desire for revenge. But as Tristan's wounds refused to heal and his body weakened, he knew in his soul that he would find no cure in Cornwall. Something called him from the depths of his being to go to sea, for only there had he a chance for healing or for death. 'You must set me in a boat and cast me on to the seas, for there I will either find a cure or I will die. But here, there is no cure for me here, only death.'

So the knights laid him in a boat, whose sails billowed in the breeze, and they pushed him into the deeper waters and the embrace of the sea. With his lyre he played sweet music for seven days and nights as he drifted he knew not where. Then fishermen heard his song and found him near their shore. When they saw his terrible wounds, they sent word to their queen. It was the queen of Ireland, who came with Iseult the Fair to watch as they carried him to the castle at Whitehaven. Iseult the Fair was the only woman who could heal his wounds, but more than any other woman in the world it was Iseult who would wish the stranger dead!

As Tristan lay sleeping, Iseult the Fair brought herbs and magic potions to cure his wounds. She saw he was of noble blood, but as he woke to her fine beauty he gave not a word away as to his true identity. None of Morholt's men recognized him, such was his pallor. His health was restored and his strength returned, and one night he crept away and found a boat that would take him across the sea and back to Cornwall.

But on Tristan's return to Tintagel with his wounds healed, the king told him that it would be impossible for him to be made heir to the throne. Many of the barons envied him, and many sought to prove he had been bewitched or was evil himself, for how could a dying man be restored from certain death on the high seas? To appease the great lords, who were still urging him to have sons, King Mark fell silent, pretending to meditate on the woman he should marry, but secretly wondering how he could still make Tristan his heir.

One day a swallow flew across the courtyard and dropped a lock of golden hair into the king's open hand. To put off the angry barons, he called them together and told them he would marry the girl whose golden hair he had just been sent from the wings of a bird.

Tristan recognized the hair instantly as that of the beautiful Iseult, the daughter of the queen of Ireland, and he offered to go back to Ireland

and ask for Iseult's hand on King Mark's behalf. For while Tristan had been in Ireland he had heard that whoever could slay the dragon would be able to take the hand of the Princess Iseult as a reward. If he slew the great beast that was terrorizing the country, perhaps the queen of Ireland would look more favourably on King Mark's proposal, especially as it might bring peace between the two kingdoms.

Tristan disguised himself as a Cornish trader and set out to slay the Irish dragon. He spent many months searching for its lair and eventually found the monster in the caves beneath the mountains. For many hours he fought in a bloody sweat, and at the last thrust of his blade the dragon fell dead. But its breath was so poisonous that it weakened Tristan, and he fell down unconscious.

The queen of Ireland and Iseult found Tristan lying beside the dragon's great steaming corpse, and they took him back to their palace to nurse him. Once again, Iseult made potions and tinctures to heal Tristan's wounds. She bathed him in herbal waters and rubbed oils into his skin until he began to recover his health. But one morning Iseult entered his bed-chamber before he woke, and she saw that his sword had fallen to the floor. As she put it back on his bed, she noticed that a piece of the gleaming metal had broken off. This missing piece was exactly the same shape as the piece she and her mother had found in Morholt's head. The piece that she had kept safely in a reliquary in the sacred chamber of the castle.

Realizing that it must have been Tristan who had killed Morholt, she cried: 'You are the Tristan who murdered my uncle! It cannot be true that you are here in my own palace.'

Iseult wanted revenge. She reached for his sword to kill him, but Tristan spoke gently, his words of love turning her heart, for now she remembered that she was to become Tristan's wife. He had slain the monster and she could not harm him.

'Listen, fair Iseult. A swallow flew into Tintagel carrying two strands of your golden hair. They brought me peace and happiness, and I travelled long to Ireland to kill the monster and find you. If you look at the golden threads upon my coat you will find two strands of your hair are sewn there, and look how golden they glow.'

Iseult was enchanted by Tristan's words. She found her golden hair among the threads of his coat of arms. For a while she remained silent, the sword placed once more upon his bed, and then she kissed him sweetly on the lips. So, as the days passed and they spent long hours in each other's company, a bond formed between them that could not be broken.

It took many days for Tristan to recover. Then, standing before the court, he told the king of Ireland his mission: that he had come to slay the dragon and claim Iseult as the bride of King Mark of Cornwall so that there could be peace between the two kingdoms and the end of all war. The Irish king was glad for the alliance and quickly agreed to the marriage to heal the rift between Ireland and Cornwall. Iseult was deeply unhappy. She had begun to feel something deeper in her heart for Tristan than she could ever imagine, but he had lied to her and tricked her into believing that he had come to Ireland for her. The wonderful story of the golden hair was just another lie. How could she love him now that he had deceived her so?

The queen noticed her daughter's great unhappiness and assumed that it was because she was to marry a man she did not know. So the sorceress gathered wild flowers and strange herbs. She brewed them in wine and with a magical spell enchanted the potion with the power of love. 'Whoever shall drink of this wine will love each other every moment of every day, with passion and desire so strong that it will not wane.' Then she sent for Brangaine, one of Iseult's maids.

'Brangaine, you must take this vessel of wine with you to Cornwall, and make sure that only Iseult and King Mark drink of it on their wedding night. If they drink of it together my daughter can be happy.' Brangaine accompanied Iseult and Tristan on the boat to Cornwall and hid the pitcher of magic potion in a secret place.

One night, as he was restlessly pacing the deck of the ship, Tristan found Iseult, her face sad and shedding tears for her home. He came to comfort her, but Iseult would not turn her head nor rest her eyes on him for fear of her feelings. 'You look lonely, Iseult. Is it Ireland you yearn for or is it the thought of marrying King Mark that makes you sad?'

Iseult would not sit with him. She rose up, thirsty and tired. 'It is nothing. The trip is long and I am in need of a sip of wine to take the chill of the night from my heart.'

Tristan bowed his head and went in search of wine. Hidden beneath the old sacking he found a pitcher of a brew that smelled mellow and seemed to be infused with cloves and herbs. He set the jug before Iseult and together they sipped it. Through the night they drank the magic potion and as each drop fell into their mouths, the power of the brew began to hold them enchanted by one another. They sat spellbound until Brangaine came and took her lady to her tent.

Tristan rose from his pallet the following morning, but only the image of Iseult's loveliness tormented his eyes. Within three days he became wretched with love. He was passionate for her touch, enflamed by burning desire and tortured by an unknown madness. Finally, he could not hold himself back and he visited her tent, knowing that he must speak the truth to her before they reached Cornwall.

'My lord, you are welcome to stay awhile.'

'Do not call me your lord, when you are my one and only queen.'

'Oh Tristan, I should have left you for dead. I should have let you die for what you did to my uncle, and now I am become your slave against my will. I did not know that I would feel this way. I did not know how tormented I should be.'

'Iseult, what is it that torments you so?'

Iseult lifted her face and the moment of desire was known to them both as she whispered, 'The love I feel for you.' Unable to hide their feelings, they made love beneath the stars as the ship rolled through the waves towards England. Even when Bragaine came upon them, she could do nothing to undo the wrong. They were tied, those lovers, in a knot that had drawn them together from eternity. A power that was not their own had chosen to mould them into one, and, realizing that the consequences of their joy could be only love or death, Tristan welcomed both, for without Iseult, he would let death come.

On the wedding night Iseult could not go through with the union with King Mark. She asked Brangaine to take her place in the royal bed so that King Mark would suspect nothing. He was drunk anyway on wine and happiness and spent the night making love to Brangaine, until she slipped away before dawn to Iseult's chamber, leaving the king snoring in a stupor of love and alcohol.

But Tristan and Iseult had met secretly that night, for there was nothing now that could keep them apart. Like a raging forest fire their love burned on, always hidden but always smouldering, always intent on its own purpose. It was as if the two hearts had been driven by some lost vision, some lost spirit of the world that left no room for their own clarity of mind. For many months they would meet in the orchards outside Tintagel, taking pleasure from one another, but always in danger of being found.

One day the fated lovers took too many chances, and they were discovered. Many of the other courtiers were jealous of Tristan's position, and when they found out that he was meeting Iseult, they did everything they could to expose his treachery. Whispers became nightmares for the king, and his suspicions began to grow as each day Iseult seemed to be less and less able to return his love.

'Through the night they drank the magic potion'

Soon the lovers had no choice but to escape, to flee from the court and from the king, who would, they knew, never forgive them when he learned of their treachery. They ran into the Forest of Morois and for

three years lived like wild animals, scavenging for roots and herbs, eating berries and wearing rabbit skins in the cold of winter. There they stayed, not knowing why they gazed at one another so, not knowing that the potion still coursed through their blood. Then, in the dark evening in their lonely clearing came a hermit, a holy man called Ogrin, who knew Tristan as soon as he set eyes upon him.

'Why do you do this, Sir Tristan? You are a traitor, and you have betrayed your king. You must return Iseult the Fair to the man to whom she is rightfully wed. Then you must make penance for your sin.'

'What crime have I committed, Ogrin? It was not my fault that I fell in love, for it was the wine that we drank upon the seas, a magical brew that has forced us to live like savages and to deceive and lie. Yet I cannot give her up, for it is an addiction of desire.'

'We do not love each other, Lord Ogrin,' implored Iseult. 'It was the potion that was sinful, not I nor he.'

Ogrin left them then, and they abandoned the clearing and went further into the forest, fearing they would be found. But one day a stealthy huntsman found their bower in the deep forest and returned to Tintagel to tell the king of their deceit. The huntsman showed King Mark the place where they lay, and he found Tristan and Iseult sleeping side by side. Between them lay Sir Tristan's sword. Mark was filled with rage and jealousy, but he knew that it was not with a mad passion that they loved one another. For the sword that lay between them was proof of their chastity. They must be pure and uncorrupted, for the sword proved them to be so! To show his forgiveness, he exchanged Tristan's sword for his own, so that the lovers would realize they had been discovered and that the king would be reconciled with them.

When they awoke, Iseult saw how the king had been merciful. But now it was not fear of the king that filled their hearts but fear of their own destiny, for the king's compassion made Tristan wonder at his actions. Overcome by remorse for what he had done, he knew that to part with Iseult and to return her to the king would be worse than death. His conscience, however, raised many questions, for Tristan wanted to be loved by his uncle and to enjoy the company and the comradeship of the court again. He also knew that Iseult was a queen, not a wild woman of the forests, and that she, too, must go where she belonged. Iseult also recalled how Tristan was wasted in the forest. She knew that he must travel and undergo adventures and the joys of knighthood, rather than languishing in the forest in terrible poverty and ill health. So the lovers agreed to leave the wild place and return to Tintagel, to make amends to the king in the hope he would welcome Iseult's return.

On the day that the lovers were to part they stayed a while in the woods. Still they would keep their vows, however far and however long they were to be apart.

'Wherever I am, whatever happens to me, fair Iseult, I shall only ever have one love. I shall only ever be yours and there will be none other.'

And Iseult gave Tristan a jasper ring. 'My friend, keep this ring always, and then if you request my presence I will come to you wherever you are, but only as long as he that comes can show me this ring, to know that it is the truth from your heart.'

So Iseult returned to Tintagel, and the land was peaceful and happy again. Yet the barons would not believe her to be good, and new fears grew in the king's heart that she was unchaste. So Iseult demanded her right to Trial of God. She was to take hold of a red-hot iron bar in her hand, and if she spoke the truth, God would not let the iron burn her, but if she lied it would sear her skin and she would be burned at the stake for treason.

Iseult sent a messenger to Tristan so that he might help her in the secret plan. On the day she was to undergo the trial, Tristan, disguised in rags as a poor beggar, arrived at the shore. The fire blazed on the beach, and the relics were placed on a sacred stone. The iron bar was set in the white of the fire, and all was ready for the test. Queen Iseult came by boat and saw the men on the shore. She pointed towards the poor pilgrim and demanded of a knight to bring him to her. 'Let that poor pilgrim carry me across the shingle and the tide so that I might arrive dry and untouched by the sand and sea.'

So Tristan lifted the queen out of her boat and waded back across the shallows to the land. He set her down on the sand, her milk-white robes flowing around her beauty, so that all who saw her stand tall and proud sighed at her grace. She clutched the relics to her heart and made an oath. 'Upon the honour of these saints, no man has ever held me in his arms apart from the king, my husband, and that poor pilgrim who brought me across the shallows from my boat.'

Then, taking the red-hot iron from the fire, her courage strong, her spirit willing, she walked forwards across the beach and cast the glowing bar of iron upon the rocks. The burning metal shrieked and hissed as it hit the water's edge, and Iseult turned to the people, raising her hands, which were still fair and white, unblemished, no signs of heat, no signs of burning. So the people wept in happiness, now sure that their queen had spoken the truth.

But Tristan still came to her window, and for many nights he could not keep himself from visiting her chamber. Iseult could not forget her oath to the king, but at each meeting when she saw Tristan's love she knew that she must go to him. Often they took pleasure from each other in the stillness of the night, but spies began to whisper again, and the queen knew they no longer had much time to love. Tearfully, Tristan bade her farewell, sensing that the only way to end his passion for Iseult was to leave this land.

Tristan fled across the seas, his aching desire still wretched in his body. In Brittany, at Carhaix, he offered arms to the king as a brave and goodly knight and as the king of Lyonesse. The king's son, Kaherdin, became a great friend of Tristan's, and together they rode out to do battle with the enemy, the traitor Count Riol. Their love and affection grew, and they became like brothers, for every combat and every battle into which they rode enhanced their fame and renewed their bravery.

Kaherdin had a sister, Iseult of the White Hands. Tristan had been startled by Iseult's name when he had first met her, weaving in the women's room. Every day Kaherdin would remind Tristan of her grace and beauty, of her gentle nature and her good intent. When Count Riol eventually surrendered, the king of Carhaix revealed that his affection for Tristan was now as deep as that of his son.

'Do me the honour, sir, to take my daughter, Iseult of the White Hands, to be yours.'

'I will, indeed, honour you, sir, and she shall be mine,' replied Tristan.

It seemed at last that Tristan had reconciled his feelings and had left behind his sadness and suffering for Iseult of Tintagel, for he loved this woman Iseult of Brittany for her grace and gentleness. Soon they were married, but on their wedding night, as Tristan removed his coat, a green jasper ring fell from his pocket to the stone floor. As the stone caught the light of the glittering candle, Tristan was filled with memories, with guilt and with a sense of betrayal. He could not forget Iseult the Fair. How could he have married another, when his heart still yearned for her? How could he lie with this woman when he had promised Iseult that he would never betray their love? And now he could not tell this fair woman about his doomed passion, for he felt only pity and sorrow at her plight, she who had done no wrong!

In the cold bed Tristan lay still and empty of feeling. Iseult must speak, for she could not bear to see him suffer so. 'Tell me, my lord, why you do not even touch my hand, nor kiss my face?'

'There was nothing now that could keep them apart'

So Tristan lied, to save her honour and to save his own. 'Once I nearly died from a great wound when in Ireland, and I swore to the Mother of God that if she healed me I would never take pleasure from any bride I married for one year. This is an oath I must not break.'

26

Poor Iseult of the White Hands nodded, and that night she cried herself to sleep, but as the days passed she could not keep her secret, for Kaherdin sensed that his sister was unwell and seemed unmoved by love or comfort. One day, as he and Tristan rode together from the castle, he demanded to know the truth.

'I cannot lie to you, good Sir Kaherdin, for you are my truest and only friend. This is the story that none but you know, save the woman to whom I owe my life and death.' Then Tristan told Kaherdin of the love potion and the passionate suffering, of the years in the Forest of Morois, of the green jasper ring and the memory of Iseult the Fair. 'I cannot live without her, for life is like death to me, it is without want nor hope, without happiness nor joy. It cannot be that I live this way for long.'

For three days Kaherdin turned to solitude to consider Tristan's plight. He felt both compassion for Tristan's dark secret and sorrow for his sister's circumstances. Then he came to Tristan's chamber and drank mead with him.

'Whatever you have done and whatever way you live now is madness; it is wrong for you, and it is wrong for my sister. Listen to my idea. You must go to Tintagel and see if the queen still feels the same way for you as you do for her. If not, then may you not grow fonder of my dear sister? But if the queen still loves you, then you must release yourself from one.'

Tristan agreed, and together Kaherdin and he travelled to Cornwall. They sent ahead the green jasper ring so that Iseult knew of his coming, but she had heard stories that Tristan had married. Her own suffering was intense. How could he have betrayed her? He had promised only ever to love her, and thus it was that she refused to see him.

Tristan returned to Carhaix in greater sadness. There seemed now no point in living. Nothing held any worth for him, and he became tortured by his rejection and full of pain. Once more, on an impulse, he set off for Tintagel, vowing to himself that he must talk with Iseult and truly know if she cared not for him. They met in the courtyard. He was disguised as a court jester, but she was overcome with desire when she saw it was he. For three nights they met in secret and made love, and now Tristan was sure that there would never be an escape from his intense passion.

'I must go, dear queen. For they will find me soon. There is only one way now, one path for us to travel down. And when I am near the end of my journey I will call for you.'

'I shall come to you wherever you are, dear Tristan.'

For many months did Tristan grieve in Carhaix. He would not touch his wife nor would he enjoy the company of others. In battle, too, his bravery diminished, and one day he was poisoned by a deadly spear.

He called Kaherdin to him, knowing that only one person could heal him now. 'Go quickly to Iseult the Fair. Take this ring and tell her she must come, for we drank the potion of love and death together. Only if she comes will I live, for I swore to serve only one love, and she knows this to be true.'

Kaherdin agreed that if he were successful in bringing Iseult back to France he would raise a white sail on the ship; if he failed to bring her he would raise a black sail.

Tristan became too ill to watch for the ship's return and asked his wife to look out for the boat. But Iseult of the White Hands had listened to their conversation, and now revenge filled her dark heart. She longed to prevent Iseult the Fair from ever seeing Tristan again. Her suspicions of Tristan's trips to England had been justified, for she had heard whispers that he had once had a lover in Cornwall.

When she saw the ship coming towards the shore, with its white flag raised, billowing against the churning winds, she ran back to the palace and found Tristan lying half-unconscious on his bed. 'The ship returns, my lord, but the flag is black!' she cried, the evil jealousy creeping into her words. And as Iseult of the White Hands stormed out of the bed-chamber, Tristan lost the will to live. Now that Kaherdin was returning without Iseult he could find no strength, no energy. Without Iseult the Fair there was no way to live, only a way to die! In a moment of complete despair, his longing for Iseult tormenting his soul, he lay back against the cold stone wall, his heart now desolate, his life gone.

From the beach where now Queen Iseult stood, she saw a flag slowly raised upon the castle ramparts. The wind picked up brightly at first, then harsh and cruel. A fisherman spoke in her ear, news she dared not believe, news that Tristan was dead. She ran up the path that led across the cold cliffs to the palace, her hair blown wild about her. Those who saw her arrive thought her beautiful. Some say she was mad with rage, others that she was sad with despair.

Beside Tristan's bed crouched Iseult of the White Hands, the wifely tears remorseful, her anger only at herself for her wretched act of revenge. Now came Iseult the Fair, sweeping past the other Iseult, her gown rustling across the stone floor and her golden hair lighting the gloomy chamber. 'Do not mourn him, lady, for I have more reason than you can ever have to do so! Understand this!'

Iseult of the White Hands, numb with grief and guilt, withdrew. Iseult the Fair lay down beside the body of Tristan and kissed his face. She pulled him to her closely and then gave up her life. Of grief she died for her friend; of grief she died for her lover.

King Mark understood their tragic ending and took the bodies of Tristan and Iseult back to Cornwall to be buried side by side, so that they could eternally be together. He planted two trees over the grave, and as they grew, the trunks began to lean towards one another and the branches intertwined, until there grew only one tree, which held the secret of the lovers' embrace locked in its tangled boughs.

Reflections

The rich and symbolic tale of Tristan and Iseult offers many ideas and concepts, both spiritual and psychological, perhaps more than it is possible to consider in the space allotted here. Robert A. Johnson, a Jungian analyst, wrote a highly acclaimed book that explored the tale of Tristan and Iseult in great detail. Together with my own less scholarly but wide-ranging observations, I should like to include some thoughts from his magnificent work. In doing so, I have, where necessary, quoted from his insights. The rich imagery and symbolism of this great and wondrous tale deserves at least a book's worth of reflections; here are but a few.

This is a myth that carries more than a tale of passion and romance, for it also carries the embryo of Western patriarchal idealism beneath its veneer of tragic and unbelievably perfect love. The dizzy, unbelievable force we feel when we fall in love is now an integral part of our Western culture, ingrained into our beings like an insect trapped in a piece of amber. It is rare and it is wondrous to fall in love, but it also carries with it danger. For this romance, this dance of energy that we believe to be the 'be all and end all' of our existence in the eyes of someone new, is in reality both an illusion and yet also a truth. The energy and the surge of profound power we feel is certainly real – this is the truth – but it is a force that has been jolted out of its alignment like a slipped disc, wrenched from its origins at a period in history when Western man needed a new meaning in life. We have projected this mysterious energy into only one place, the eyes of another human being. This mystery, this falling in love is none other than a moment of divine contact with the inner world of self. We fall in love with ourselves, but we do not see ourselves projected strangely in front of us on another person through our one-way vision eyes. Why this actually happens and what the trigger is for such a moment is the mystery. But precisely because it is a mystery means that it is one of the richest and one of the most powerful energies that rise up in the human psyche, whether it comes to us in the form of spiritual awakening or romantic longing.

Courtly love developed between the end of the ninth century and the beginning of the fourteenth century. The early Christian church had attempted to show women as sinful, especially as regards their sexuality. It was out of this bleak view from the Dark Ages that visionaries, mystics, poets and writers aspired to courtly love, a mixture of both the spirit of Catharism and the mystical beliefs that the Crusaders brought back with them from the East.

It was an inspirational and perhaps often maligned sub-culture that, to begin with, attempted to induce divine love out of human form, and then later, as trade routes opened up the exotic worlds of the Middle East and the esoteric secrets of transformative love, to draw together erotic and sacred sexuality. Women were idealized and loved from afar; they were physically unblemished, and their purity was unquestionable, in theory at least. Romance filled the gap between spiritual ecstasy and profane sexuality. If that moment of ecstasy could remain and the heightening of sensation linger, suffering and pain would be transcended. Romantic love shone out as a beacon to the Western psyche, and particularly the Western patriarchy, which demanded that women be seen only in a context that ensured that men were in control. To put a woman on a pedestal, to spiritualize her, meant that her reality, her earthy, dark, sexual feminine qualities could easily be ignored or suppressed. The intellectualization of courtly love was essentially, in theory at least, a way out of man's own lusty dilemma; a way of avoiding or confronting their own sexual needs, or as they saw it the temptation of women. But paradoxically, the passions that were awakened also became the great price that love must pay. The erotic and the divine merged under the bedcovers of this intellectualization. Far from the ideal theory of courtly love becoming an abstract sacred expression, it appears that many Crusaders brought back sexual tantric skills from the East to compliment their more lofty aspirations.

Thus esoteric medieval courtly love relied on the fact that man could attain divine love through the earthly love of women. So it was that a woman provided love, sexual bliss and, of course, the transformation of the man's soul through her body. Many of the women poets and writers of the medieval period could allude to the physical passion and the sexual desire of courtly love only through the symbolism and allegory of their words; but so much more was occurring under the bedcovers than was ever believed.

This change in the image of woman and of romantic love in Western history is something we carry today as part of our archetypal heritage. As Robert A. Johnson reminds us in *We: Understanding the Psychology of Romantic Love*:

> It still hasn't occurred to Western man to stop looking on woman as the symbol of something, and to begin seeing her simply as a woman – as a human being. He is caught in the ambivalence he feels towards his own inner feminine.

31

Today we assume that one other person can fulfil us, can give us everything, be everything and carry our burdens for us. We confuse romance with sex and love; we commit ourselves only to our own passions, not to another human being. Robert Johnson also nudges us to remember that Tristan and Iseult:

> do not actually love each other. They use each other as vehicles to
> have the intense, passionate experiences they long for.

The love potion is perhaps the closest symbol for the moment of falling in love we can possibly have. Something mysterious happens; ingredients blend, are brewed and an alchemical reaction occurs. This moment of 'falling' is exactly that. We fall into the potion and then find it very difficult to get out. It drugs us, as it did Tristan and Iseult for three years, intoxicates us so that we are unaware of anything else in our life. The potion pulls us further in, we fall down the well of apparent happiness only to find a black pit filled with suffering and illusion. Reality is distorted, 'me' becomes more important than 'you' – my desires, my needs, my passion. We live for passion only; the addictive dark cries from the unconscious easily surge up into the light of day and overwhelm us with a feeling of ecstasy. Enlightenment then release – these are moments that cannot be denied, and we all have experienced them as such.

Tristan and Iseult feel they have a right to their affair in that the magic potion is to blame. Falling in love happens to us, we do not make it happen. And often it is the magic potion that becomes an excuse for romantic love when a third party may be involved.

King Mark represents strength, security and gentleness, and Iseult of the White Hands represents the earth-mother, the nurturing, supportive woman who genuinely and compassionately cares about another human being. Both these characters symbolize the gentle, human qualities of our existence. Tristan and Iseult can never participate in this while they are caught up in the existential partitioning of romance.

So why cannot these two lovers let go of one another? Simply because they do not want to let go! The pain and the suffering, the despair and the agony are what make them feel truly alive! The love potion poisons them, but it poisons not only their hearts; it throws its acidic elements into their eyes so that they become blinded by the light of their expectations.

This is where idealization of one person, of expectations and commitment to passion only, means there is little room for real human love. We have become confused about our quest for a meaning in life, and this is why romantic love has provided an easy alternative and an excuse for selfish desires, for our own fires to burn unchecked in our souls. For 'a power that was not their own had chosen to mould them into one'.

Tristan and Iseult are not real, but they carry for us those very apparent 'real' desires that seem to come from nowhere and possess us from the moment the wondrous but deadly potion takes effect. This possession sweeps us along until the broom cannot hold any more dust and we begin to question where we are going and, more importantly, who it is that is going with us.

Conscience, morality and humankindness appear in the guise of Ogrin, the holy hermit, and Kaherdin, the sensible side-kick who jolts Tristan into an awareness of basic human necessity. The arrival of King Mark and his laying down of his sword between the two sleeping lovers begins the test, the moment when in our own modern-day love affairs we begin to review, often unconsciously, our impulses, our projections and our motivations. We cut through our illusions with the swords of rational, but sometimes equally dangerous, assumptions. Something changes, something stirs deep within, and the quest for that intense buzz of profound romantic ecstasy begins to be usurped with a sense that something else is lacking. Mark's compassion brings both guilt and deep inner reflection to Tristan's suffering. For whether it is romantic or spiritual love that we seek, we cannot carry on this inner journey at the expense and exile of genuine human love.

If Tristan, and many other lovers like him, could freely and unconditionally let go of Iseult, let go of the desire and the commitment he has to his own passion, he might experience both divine and human love on a more balanced set of scales.

Romantic love is a beautiful and mysterious energy, and if we can allow ourselves that awareness, we can enjoy such moments without suffering, without blame and mostly without such high expectations of another human being. In our contemporary Western world we often say 'I'm not in love with you any more' and think that this must be the ending of a relationship. But if we can reclaim the projection consciously, and value it as well as still valuing the other upon whom we initially assigned this force, this moment may actually be the precursor to a valuable unconditional love for others.

The Death-stone

Origins and Traditions

RECORDS of ancient Japanese mythology are sparse. The earliest Shinto peoples had a mythology filled with beings, spirits and ghosts of every imaginable kind, yet by the fourth century CE Japan had opened up to religious and cultural influences from mainland China. Japanese mythology quickly absorbed both Buddhist philosophy and the gods and supernatural deities that came direct from China and from India.

The fox is a well-documented shape-shifter spirit in both Chinese and Japanese mythology. In China the power to turn into a fox means you are able to acquire immortality, and legends abound concerning the supernatural powers of the fox. These spirits have the power of infinite vision and all-encompassing knowledge, which they acquire by dabbling in the classical and erudite literature of all civilizations. Their wisdom enables them to shape-shift from fox to man, from man to fox. They can transmute, and they can delude. In Japanese mythology the fox, known as Kitsune, is malicious, although the Inari fox is the messenger of the god of harvest.

In Chinese Taoist belief, foxes can steal another human being's life essence, thereby adding to and improving their own. This is usually done during sexual intercourse. An essential component in the Chinese Taoist belief in attaining immortality relied on the union of male and female. If one partner experienced an orgasm, and the other partner restrained him or herself, the life essence from the first was absorbed into the other.

Fox-spirits will often take the form of a beautiful woman to extract a man's life essence during sexual intercourse, thus adding to their own potency and energy in order to achieve immortality. The more men a fox-woman can seduce and the more men who reach orgasm, the more they will lose some of their life essence and the more hers will increase. The only way you can know if you are in the company of a fox-woman is to watch for her shadow on water. A fox-spirit's reflection will be cast as the outline of a fox, not as the woman you see before you.

This myth is about a shape-shifter spirit who lures the mikado into a deadly trap of love and treachery to empower itself with life essence and subsequent immortality.

The Myth

A VERY long time ago there was a Buddhist priest called Genno. After many days spent travelling, he was overcome with exhaustion, and he went to rest under the shadow of a great stone on Nasu Moor. He was just about to lie down and place his head against the soft sand at the base of the stone when a cloud-spirit suddenly swirled into a formless being before him. 'You must not rest under this stone, dear priest, for this is the Death-stone. Every man, beast or bird that has touched it has instantly died!'

The priest immediately sat up, convinced that the spirit's warning was genuine. His curiosity was now aroused, and just as the spirit was about to disappear he urged the being to tell him more about the Death-stone.

'Please, do me the honour of telling me how this terrible stone came to be so. I am in need of company and a drink from the pool before I continue on my way.'

So the spirit began: 'Many full moons ago there was a beautiful girl who lived at the court of Japan. She was so exquisite – eyes as green as jade, hair the colour of a million ravens – and she was called the Jewel Maiden. Her wisdom was as incredible as her beauty. She was educated in Confucian classics, and in all the poetry and sciences of China as well as of Japan. No other woman displayed such wonderful qualities or could rival her for looks or skills, and she had soon enchanted the mikado's heart.

'The mikado lusted after the Jewel Maiden and arranged a great feast at the Summer Palace where he could finally tell her of his desire for her. He invited all the wisest, wealthiest, wittiest and most important people in the land, including the Jewel Maiden herself. The court was filled with music, with food and drink, with laughing and brilliant minds. The feast included the best delicacies, and the music was the sweetest ever heard. But as the evening turned to night, dark clouds gathered across the court. The sky became dark, blackened by fast-moving shadows that scudded across the stars until there were none left to see. The night became pitch black. Then suddenly a strange wind whistled through the court and many of the guests sat rigid with fear. Others ran out of the court only to find they were in complete blackness. Then, amid the chaos and the confusion, one guest cried out, "I see a light! Look, a light!"

'The gathered revellers stared at a mysterious spark, darting and sparkling into a flame from the centre of the Jewel Maiden's body. The light seemed to emanate from within the Jewel Maiden and gradually to glow throughout her whole being. The mikado felt himself hypnotized to go to her, unable to resist her dazzling gaze. The light pierced every corner of the palace, and the brilliant glow forced every person to turn their eyes away. Some looked down at the floor, others covered their eyes with their hands, and others fell into a heap on the floor. After some minutes the light began to die down. It grew smaller, losing its luminous power until the sparkling flames disappeared back inside the Jewel Maiden's body. The mikado was dazed, for somehow he knew he had been enchanted. While the glorious light had shone throughout the court he had found himself in a physical embrace of such ecstasy with the Jewel Maiden that he had been empowered and exhausted by her sexual artistry. As the Jewel Maiden slipped quietly from the great feasting hall, the mikado remembered his moments of passion. "Where is she? Where has the Jewel Maiden gone?" he cried, suddenly aware of her disappearance.

'"It is no use, my lord, the Maiden has gone. We do not know where, for no one saw her go."

'Within hours the mikado became very ill. He developed a fever and lay thrashing in a delirium of love-sickness until the court magician arrived. The magician frowned as the mikado refused to eat or drink, and he finally nodded to the gathered courtiers. "This is the doing of the

The Mikado had been enchanted by the Jewel Maiden

37

wicked Jewel Maiden. She has captured his life essence. The light that appeared to you all at the feast has drawn the mikado's own inner potency from him."

'The mikado tossed and turned in despair, for not only did he still long for the Jewel Maiden but he now knew that she had drained all his pleasure from him. He would never be able to enjoy love again. Floundering in his impotence and his desire for the Jewel Maiden, he vowed never to speak to any woman again.

'The Jewel Maiden returned to the palace the next evening, hoping that the mikado would remember their passion together. Hungry to drain more of his sexual power from him, she pleaded with the courtiers to let her pass. "I have come to see the mikado. I know that he loves me."

'"You are not welcome," replied the mikado's sister. "He is ill with desire for you, but he refuses to see you for he believes you have powers that can do him much harm."

'Once the Jewel Maiden knew the mikado's suspicions, she turned herself into her original form and ran as fast as she could away from the palace. The fox-woman ran and ran until she reached Nasu Moor, and here she came to rest at this very stone.'

The priest frowned curiously at the spirit's story. 'It is you, isn't it?'

The spirit nodded. 'Yes, I am the demon-spirit that once dwelt in the soul of the Jewel Maiden, and now I live in the Death-stone for ever!'

The priest was shocked and slightly fearful at the blatant revelation of the spirit, but he knew that, as a priest, he had no right to judge.

'You have found great wickedness in your spirit, but you can find great virtue also. Take this begging bowl and priestly robe and reveal your true fox form to me.'

But the spirit wailed pitifully that it could not do so, and immediately vanished into thin air. Genno was not put off by the weakness of the spirit, and so that it might attain Nirvana he burned incense, offered flowers and recited the Buddhist scriptures before the stone. He bowed his head and then spoke: 'Now, spirit of the Death-stone, come to me and tell me how you came to be this demon.'

Suddenly the stone burst open and the spirit appeared, shimmering from the centre of the rock. The air turned a lurid green, and the light swirled like a luminous mist around Genno until it transformed into the fox. For only a few seconds did the fox gaze at Genno, its eyes bright with desire, with the power of all the emperors of Japan stored in its hungry heart. Then, suddenly, the fox changed again into a beautiful girl and was able to speak.

'In this form, as a woman, I have caused much unhappiness and tried to destroy the Imperial line. I have slept with many emperors in order to take their life essence, to end their potency. Then I went to the court of the great mikado, and I seduced him, too. But I returned because I believed I had found great affection for this mortal man, and I returned to offer him my love. But the mikado's sister prevented me from seeing him, for he had found out my secret, I know not how. So I ran from the palace and came to this moor, where I have stayed ever since, haunting those who come by. But now the Lord Buddha has come to give me a chance to make peace with myself, but I can do so only if I return forever to this stone.'

It was too late for Genno to stop her, and as quickly as she had come to him in his world, she left it. The cloud of swirling colours and the beautiful maiden before him transformed back for a second into a fox, which smiled, then finally into a formless demon, a wisp of black smoke that struggled as the great Death-stone sucked the spirit back into the solid rock forever.

Reflections

The power of this myth lies in the strange mixture of Buddhist belief and the ancient, more pagan earth magic of the shape-shifting fox. Yet it is spiritual love, in the form of a Buddhist priest, that manages to conquer the deadly seductive qualities of the shape-shifting spirit.

The Death-stone is an image of solidity and power itself. But 'if you lie beneath or beside this place you will surely die,' says the spirit, who has been banished to this lonely and desolate place. But would the priest really have died or was this fearful story just the spirit's way of amusing itself? How many travellers have stopped there and been told the same tale, and how many of the travellers end up being lured into a more sinister trap of having their own 'life essence' absorbed by this treacherous creature?

In much of Japanese and Chinese art huge boulders and rocks and great stones standing alone are symbols of yang energy – that is, strong, assertive, active and dynamic. Yet here, in this solid and usually reliable place, we come face to face with the dark side of our own instinctive nature. The power to take from others what is not ours. It is often when we are most sure, most convinced, most proud, most reliable that we unconsciously feed off other people's values, warmth, love and receptiveness. Unwittingly, we become like the spirit held by the rock, hungry for life's potency, feeding and sucking every drop of our partner's or lover's own inner resources. A seemingly powerful and dynamic partner, like the rock, can often conceal behind its firm and resolute face a demanding, greedy and undermining nature, often as compensation for an inner vulnerability.

So the Death-stone symbolizes the power of concealment and becomes a stone of endings. It is a place where we should feel safe and where we should be able to rest and lay our weary head like the traveller, but it is also a place filled with a willfulness driven by insecurity.

Genno, the priest, does not become tempted by the divine form of a woman he sees before him nor is he seduced by the sad tale the spirit tells of its doomed existence. This part of our psyche, the part within that knows the difference between goodness and evil intention, knows that the spirit has done wrong but allows also for compassion. Buddhist philosophy is about compassion and suffering, and this tale nudges us to remember that if we empathize, if we care about those who are greedy, demanding, insufferable and filled with hatred, the energy of human love may at least empower the Death-stone's spirit with a new faith.

Etain and Midhir

Origins and Traditions

THE mythology of the Celtic races is, like its people, fragmented and scattered across a great part of Europe. Many stories appear in different forms, adapted to the diverse cultures and smaller communities wherever these peoples settled.

The early origins of the Celtic race developed from a warrior people in eastern Europe about 2000 BCE. Apart from the Greek and Roman civilizations of the south, these early peoples dominated Europe for over 1000 years, particularly in the north and west. Most Celtic mythology was unrecorded, as it evolved as an oral tradition adapted to the movements of individual communities. It was only in about the fifth century CE, when Christianity began to seep through the Roman Empire, that monks took the trouble to write down the Celtic sagas.

In Ireland especially the Celts preferred the oral tradition to that of recorded writings. The widespread adoption of Christianity forced the Irish gods underground, and it was only through poetry and monastic literature that ancient myths were still accessible without being seen as pagan. The last gods to rule Ireland were the Tuatha Dé Danann (the people of the goddess Dana), ancient deities descended from the earth goddess common to most Celtic peoples. In Ireland these deities were overthrown by the invasion of the Milesians, the sons of a Spanish soldier known as Milesius, who apparently organized the invasion of Ireland that led to the gods being driven underground. After their defeat, the gods lived on beneath grassy mounds in glittering subterranean palaces filled with magical riches and acquired almost fairy-like qualities.

Most Irish Celtic mythology is concerned with warriors and heroes, whose own stories were born from the fierce fighting spirit of the peoples themselves. Love rarely appears within this wide-ranging mythology, and when it does it is harsh, basic and often cruel. It seems likely that the written records of those fifth-century monks dispensed with the earlier connections to the mother goddess. However, Dana or Danu (the mother goddess of the Danann), and various other goddesses, such as Boann, the water-goddess, and Cliodhna, the goddess of beauty who fell in love with a mortal, have retained their place in Irish mythology.

The following tale of reincarnation, rejection, jealousy and choice carries all the flavours of the fierce desire for mortality, and the ambivalent force of the gods. It perhaps also symbolizes the change to mortal rule that took place when the Irish gods were overcome by the Milesians. Here, Etain, a beautiful goddess, becomes reincarnated as a mortal, who must chose between her love for a mortal man and a god. Etain was one of the 'people of the goddess Danann', and this is the story of how a mortal king and a passionate god fought for her beauty and love, and of the choice she had to make.

The Myth

MIDHIR, the son of Dagdar, was refined and noble-hearted. Neither warrior skills nor combat tempted him, but brave speech, magic and the arts were those elegances that his eye and his heart were drawn towards. It was the time when the Tuatha dé Danann ruled Ireland, and Dagdar, father of all the gods, had seen those across the waters, the Fomorii, the terrifying demons of the sea, defeated by the swords of the enchanted young gods.

In Midhir's palace delight and happiness had come to him for but a short while. So bedazzled had he been by the fair, tumbling hair and wide green eyes of Fuamnach that he had married her, perhaps too soon, some said. Yet fate brought new beauty before Midhir, and such were his longings when he caught sight of the lovely goddess Etain, who clutched the bejewelled cup of plenty to her, that he was overwhelmed with love. Midhir had been married to Fuamnach for some time, yet the grace, poise and beauty of princess Etain fulfilled all his dreams. Unbuckling the fine golden clasp so that his wide cloak fell like hawk wings around his feet, he ran to the palace feast, knowing that Etain was to be a guest there. Like a child, he ran past Fuamnach, the burning flames of desire eating her black mood as he passed her by.

Midhir and Etain spoke briefly across the table, their fingers almost touching as they raised their goblets to toast Dagdar's victories in battle. Midhir took the last hazelnut from the bowl and offered it to Etain, so that she might grate its flavour upon her wine.

'Kind sir, you do me the honour of sharing this, yet I must insist that you return your favours only to your wife, she who is good and true.'

'And what if you were to become my wife, too? Is there not an unwritten law that allows me to have more than one wife? I, who have made a mistake, would now ask only to be your lord as well as your friend.'

Etain bowed her head, yet still her eyes raised to his and their bond was sealed. So Midhir arranged that he might marry Etain, and she readily agreed, knowing only how much she loved him. She kept her fears of Fuamnach's presence a well-guarded secret. But jealousy crept quickly like a cockroach into Fuamnach's heart, for she had magic spells of her own. Unrelenting and remorseless, she carried out rituals to trap Etain in the storm-winds that shared her power. Ghostly white was the wedding chamber in the candlelight that wedding night; great swathes of muslin hung from the high stone walls, billowing like clouds in the breeze. Etain turned to the window that faced the sea, and waited for her lord. On her throat was a necklace of purple stones and about her head was a garland of sweet flag irises, woven into the tangled locks of her golden hair.

She looked down upon the great loch and a vision rose to meet her, not of her lord, not of Midhir's love, but of Fuamnach's face, full of hatred and vile murmurings. The moment lingered as the weeds of a deep rock pool seemed to touch her and lull her eyes to close. Midhir entered the room aroused and ready to take his love for the first time, and yet as he ran to her arms she dissolved like a dream. Etain vanished, transformed by the evil power of Fuamnach into a deep, still pool.

For many days Midhir searched in vain for Etain, then, when it seemed that she was gone forever he halted his horse beside a still pool from which the beast would not drink.

'Midhir! Midhir! It is I! It is I!' whispered a voice across the rippled surface of the dark pool. Joyfully, Midhir plunged his hands into the pool; if he could drink of the water he might have power enough himself to bring Etain back into her divine form. Yet Fuamnach's evil was greater than his love, and as he placed his hands in the clear water the pool vanished and only a worm fell from his muddy fingers. Now a worm, Etain wriggled in the grass to hide from the thrush that saw her. Midhir knew her to be the worm, but Fuamnach in her fire of powerful magic saw Midhir reach for the worm and again transformed Etain, this time into a butterfly. As the breeze lifted, Midhir felt his cloak wrap darkly across his back, and the black skies began to grow wild across the horizon. He reached for the butterfly, but the wind lifted it fiercely into the air, away across the hills so that he had no time to follow.

The storm winds blew Etain, the butterfly, out into the wilderness of Erin. For many years she was at the mercy of the elements as storms blew her fine, fragile wings further and further away from Midhir. Then one day a gentle breeze lifted her fluttering form into the palace of an Ulster chief called Etar. This mortal's wife drank wine from a goblet as she spun her threads to weave. But, unbeknownst to Etar, the butterfly fell into this woman's wine, and Etain was swallowed. Now Fuamnach's jealous heart could do no more, for Etain would be reincarnated as a mortal, all memory of her past life as a goddess, as one of the people of Danann, forgotten; all thoughts, all feelings of her true love Midhir would be in an instant gone!

Thus Etain was born a mortal, the daughter of Etar. She knew nothing of her past life as a goddess, nor did she remember how she had once been Midhir's virgin bride. So Etain grew up to be a beautiful and much admired young woman.

About this time the high king of Ireland, Eochy, was beginning to look for a suitable wife to be his queen. He had heard much from travelling musicians of Etain's beauty and how she was the most exquisite woman in the land. One day Eochy travelled beyond his own kingdom in a vain hope of meeting the fair Etain. Through forests and over mountains he roamed, uncertain where she was and knowing only that the vision of her loveliness was haunting him so. After many miles on horseback, he grew weary and stopped to rest beside a pool.

He heard laughing and singing, the voices of women humming like honey bees beyond the trees. Fearful that he might cause alarm, he crept alongside the pool, his urgency to see who sweetly sang, forcing him to his knees as he crouched beneath the hanging boughs of ivy. When Eochy saw Etain and two other princesses swimming and diving in the deep end of the sunlit pool, he fell instantly in love with her. Hair that was like golden eaves of corn fell loosely down her back, and her skin, whiter than the most fragrant of lilies, was untouched by any other. In his passion and delirious desire, he stayed for some weeks near Etar's palace. The king welcomed him as a friend and showed pleasure that Eochy might wish the hand of his fair and most beautiful of daughters. 'Sir, it is with my blessing that you may ask Etain to wed you, for I would be honoured to know she returns to Tara with you.'

Eochy bowed his head. 'There is no other woman in Ireland whom I would wish to wed. I hope that she will allow me to court her thus.'

Then Eochy left the court. Each day he came to Etain's chambers and courted her as he was supposed to do. She began to have a genuine fondness for Eochy, but yet there was no passion blazing in her own heart, as there was in his. Kind as she was, Etain allowed him no access to her heart, but his offer of marriage was one that she could not refuse nor dare to turn down for fear of hurting his feelings. So it was that Eochy married Etain and took her back to Tara.

But now at Tara, Eochy's brother, Ailill, also fell in love with the beautiful Etain. He became so love-sick for her that he fell gravely ill and was very near to death. Eochy had many travels to make that summer throughout Ireland, and he asked Etain to look after his brother and nurse him, hoping he would not die while he was away.

Etain visited Ailill that eve of midsummer, for it was the turning of the season and the woodland doves sat upon the great stone wall cooing at the moon's silver face. Etain carried herbal potions, not knowing that Ailill was wretched with desire for her. She filled his goblet with the remedies and sat beside his bed as he awoke from a great dream. Those dull grey eyes filled with longing, for here was Etain beside him. He pulled himself from his bed and whispered to her lovely face.

'It is moments like this, Etain, when you are so close to me that I feel I must surely die if I cannot have you in body and in soul.'

Etain was surprised by his fearless words, yet she took his hand, her warm heart filled with compassion and sadness for this dying man. She knew she could never love Ailill, but nor did she want him to die of love for her.

'How can I give you my love, dear Ailill? Eochy is away, and this may be the only chance that I can return your love and prevent you from your death. Tell me what it is you want from me?'

'Meet me tomorrow in the enchanted copse. No one will see us, and there we can unite our love.'

Etain nodded, but as she left him, the joy of saving his life did not stay long with her. The guilt of her betrayal to Eochy began to weigh heavily in her heart.

Etain's rendezvous was to become a far more mysterious affair. For Ailill fell into a deep enchanted sleep on the day of their meeting. As he lay in his spellbound dream, a breeze softly fluttered across his forehead and a strange and beautiful spirit took possession of his soul. Taking his form, this spirit rose up from the bed and went to meet Etain.

Etain made her way through the tangled wood, towards the enchanted copse. When she was a child she had heard of the place and its magical powers and learned that here, no matter how little you loved someone, you would be cast under such a powerful spell that you would have no choice but to love them back.

The sunlight glinted through the dancing leaves. But the magic seemed to be broken, for Etain's heart sank when she saw the young Ailill standing beside the tree. Yet as he spoke she sensed something was not right, that some great mystery had taken over his weak and frail character.

'Dear lady, it is good that you came. But my fever, my wretchedness is nothing to do with you. I have been wrong to mislead you, and I am sorry to have put you under such an oath as to save me with love. This is as wrong for you as it is for me. Do you forgive me?'

He smiled and took her hand, and as Etain looked deep into his eyes she caught the memory of another love from some time past. Then it was gone. 'Of course, I forgive you. But you must rest, and perhaps we can at least be friends. Perhaps I can visit you again tomorrow and make sure you are well.'

'That would be wonderful, dear lady. Come to me in my chamber again, and I will make you some food and we will talk.'

He kissed her hand and she fled quickly, for fear that the magic place might suddenly entrap her in love for him.

Discomfort and mistrust grew in Etain's heart each time she visited Ailill. It was almost as if it was not he whom she was nursing but something or someone whose power and greatness was beyond her imagination. At first, he had made her food and showed her his books and journals. Then each day he grew ill with fever again, and yet there was always a strange gleam in his eyes that he could not hide.

One day, after Etain had washed his sweat-sodden clothes and made a potion to cleanse Ailill's body, she sank down on a stone seat to rest. Ailill's white face seemed for ever to fill her only with pity and compassion, yet how could she leave him now, while he suffered so? Suddenly there came a mist of fine gold that shimmered before her in the air. Above

Aillil's bed it swirled like a golden shower of rain, until it turned into the most beautiful mortal form Etain had ever seen. This was Midhir, the bold and dashing god transformed before her eyes, and she saw the soul of supernatural desire before her.

The only means of escape for Etain was to run out of the chamber. This god who appeared before her had been the same one who had come to her in the copse, with the same desire, the same love for her stirring in his eyes, so that she had remembered a time, remembered a feeling that was reawakened in her heart for this god. Not for Ailill, nor for Eochy – only for this god.

'Wait, dear Etain, you must listen to me. Do not leave in haste for you must know why I have come here in this guise.'

Etain turning, flashing her fiery eyes at the dazzling god as she sought his explanation.

'You are Etain, daughter of the great goddess, Danann. You are a goddess, too, by right. You were my wife, my love. Yet you were changed into a butterfly by the evil powers of my first wife, and must now live out this incarnation as a mortal.'

'Sir, I do not remember this, how can I remember this? Are you lying to me?' she cried, not wanting to know the truth, nor daring to question her own disbelief.

Midhir begged her to return to Erin. 'Come back with me, Etain. You loved me once, you were my bride. But we never made love because of the treachery of Fuamnach. Please return with me, because it is only you that I have searched for and longed for.'

Etain shook her head, not knowing if he was telling the truth, nor even if she wanted to leave. He followed her then out into the clear air, where the leaves dropped their morning dew upon her golden hair. She sat beside the pool of plenty and he knelt at her feet. As Midhir told her more and more about her past life, the memories of their love slashed deep into her heart like a knife. Her predicament was indeed terrible. If she visited the real Ailill again his passionate love for her would be restored, for the spell that the god had cast over him would now be shattered if she did not go with Midhir. Ailill might live if she left him now, but if she stayed he would die of love for her. And what of Eochy? She loved him with goodness and compassion, with companionship and duty, but not with the same feelings that had been stirred in her heart by this god, Midhir.

There seemed to Etain only one way to ensure that she did not hurt Eochy nor deepen Ailill's despair, to return to her past life with Midhir, but there had to be one condition.

'My lord,' she began, knowing that he would be angered by her refusal. 'There is only one condition that I ask. I shall return with you, but only if Eochy agrees to my departure. He is my mortal husband, and I love him as duty and obedience says I must. You must allow me that right.'

Midhir nodded. Then taking Etain to him, he kissed her lips without saying a word and vanished into the golden mist that had risen around the turquoise pool.

But as the days went by Etain still dared not ask Eochy if she might go. In Erin Midhir became restless, frustrated and impatient for Etain's return. The evil Fuamnach had long since died, and his passion for Etain grew so intense that he could wait no longer. Forcing Eochy into agreeing to Etain's departure was the only solution for him now.

Midhir came to King Eochy one day upon his return to the Hill of Tara and asked if he would like to play a game of chess. Eochy was honoured by the god. He loved playing chess and enjoyed gambling with his own wealth, mainly because he usually won. Midhir was unusually ineffective and allowed Eochy to win every game. In payment for all his losses Midhir was over-generous with his magical powers and vowed to restore pathways, reclaim lands and clear the forests of Tara. Eochy began to believe that he was the better player and announced rather recklessly at the beginning of the final confrontation that the stakes would be decided by the winner, but not until the end of the game. Midhir nodded. This time he won, much to Eochy's horror.

Eochy sighed, knowing he had been foolishly over-confident. He had no choice: 'What is it that you desire from me?'

Midhir laughed: 'Only that I can hold Etain in my arms and have just one kiss from her beautiful lips.'

The king was angry, but he could only nod his head. 'This will be granted to you, but do not come until one month from this day.' Eochy spent the next four weeks planning how to keep Midhir out of his kingdom. He sent armies of his men to surround the palace, and, feeling sure that one god could never infiltrate the most powerful army on earth, he invited many lords to a celebratory feast.

Etain sat beside Eochy at that feast. Long had she waited to find the courage to speak with the kind king, and yet each time she had opened her lips to tell him about Midhir she could only remember how dearly he cared for her. But then, as she sipped the feasting wine, her mouth turned to a smile at last, and the wine that clung to her lips looked like liquid jewels of desire. But it was not for Eochy that she smiled.

Suddenly Midhir appeared at the table, more radiant, more glorious than ever before. When Etain saw him, she remembered how she loved him when she too was divine. Now her own predicament had come to haunt her. Eochy or Midhir, how could she ever chose between two such powerful and passionate loves? Midhir clutched his spear in one hand and with the other hand suddenly pulled Etain to him and kissed her on the lips in front of the feasting guests. As Etain turned to acknowledge his embrace, they rose together in the air and like white eagles soared through the high arched windows out into the swirling mists. Eochy and his warriors ran outside to try and stop them, but all they could see were two white birds flying through the sky across the mountains.

Eochy was heart-broken and could not accept the fact that Etain had gone forever. For many months he travelled wearily across Ireland, looking for her in vain. He was relentless in his search and summoned the druid Dalan to use his magical powers to help him find Etain. Dalan made three wands from a yew tree, and on these wands he wrote magic spells until the yew bark burned away to reveal the place they could find Etain. The words that burned across the yew wands spelt out Bri-Leith, the palace of Midhir.

Eochy gathered his great armies together in a massive attack to destroy the palace of Midhir at Bri-Leith. When Midhir heard of Eochy's plan of attack he offered to give up Etain only if Eochy could choose the right Etain out of the fifty women he would send out beyond the palace walls. For Midhir knew that Eochy would surely die; his armies would never be strong enough for the power of the gods. Eochy sent a message in agreement, and Midhir turned to the lovely Etain and told her what she must do.

'You know the king loves you, Etain, and it is his right to come for you, who are still a mortal.'

'But I love only you, Midhir, only you, sir, can raise my soul above the mortal pain that I must bear.'

Midhir smiled upon her tears, his own held back as he spoke again. 'Yet while you are a mortal, you must love as a mortal. This king can teach you many things of love that I cannot.' And Etain then understood that her lover knew what best would feed her heart.

When he saw the fifty identical Etains walking towards him, Eochy was wretched. How could he ever chose the right Etain when the appearance of such loveliness was all the same? Dancing before her so proudly, so full of spirit, was the king's horse. The wild stallion had been tamed by the great king with love and gentleness, and it was at that moment Etain's human love for the king shone out through her sad eyes. Then Eochy jumped down off his stallion and took Etain in his arms. This was not passion nor desire, but warmth and understanding that bled like liquid gold through his sinews. Midhir saw this human love, a love that he could not feel. Knowing that he could no longer break the mortal bond of earthly love between Etain and Eochy, he vanished from Bri-Leith to return to the land of Erin.

Etain would always love Midhir with the greatest of all desire, knowing now who she had once been. One day she would be with Midhir in Erin, a goddess again. Yet now she must go to Tara to complete her mortal life with the great King Eochy.

Reflections

This tale closely echoes the mythological change from the Celtic governance of the gods and goddesses in Ireland to the mortal kings and descendants of those deities. It carries both the flavour of the transformation in supremacy from god to mortal, and the patriarchal need to assert power in the minds and hearts of brave warriors and courageous kings.

It must be remembered that this myth, as written down by monks, may well have been also an attempt to reshape the image of the great goddess to fall in line with Christianity.

Midhir seems childlike in his godly power compared with the mortals in this story, and yet it is only Midhir, the god, who can love Etain in the way she desires. Symbolically, romance and falling in love are those moments when we are most delightfully in the hands of the gods. Moments we would want and would prefer to last forever.

Etain is a goddess and is thus already in the hands of the gods, yet from the very beginning of the tale there is little chance that a simple tale of happiness will be resolved. Etain is denied an equal relationship with Midhir from the outset. Like many tragic love stories, Midhir is already married. He can still offer Etain his love, but she must pay the price.

As in many stories, Etain's reincarnation as a mortal is a necessary device to illustrate the falling from grace. So that she can learn there is more to love than the divine qualities it seems to offer, her journey must be one of suffering. Her transformation into a human means that she must suffer the needs of humanity if she is ever to regain the eternal love of a god and to become acquainted with her real self.

Etain's three incarnations – as a pool, a worm and a butterfly – are also symbolic of the process she must go through to attain a sense of human compassion. The first transformation wrought by the jealous powers of Midhir's wife, Fuamnach, is into a pool, which suggests that Etain must first become aware of the deep feelings a human being possesses. As a pool, she learns to find out about emotion. Water has always been a symbol of the deep undercurrents of our inner landscape. When Midhir attempts to drink her, she 'gets in touch with mortal feeling' and is wretchedly changed into a worm, to know what it is to be part of the earth, to be humiliated, humbled, and human. These words have the same root, the Latin word *humus* (earth). Sometimes we forget that we are part of this earth and must learn to accept nature's cycles.

The final transformation to a human can take place only when Etain is swallowed in her butterfly form. The butterfly, perhaps more poignantly than any other insect, suggests the frailty and sensitivity of love. How easy it is to be consumed by another's power and how easily a butterfly's wings crumple. We are often at the mercy of others, but although our butterfly wings are crushed, our resolve is strengthened.

As a human, Etain must now suffer the fate of all mortals, the conflict between romantic desire and human compassion. Compassion means 'with suffering', and this feeling of empathy with another is what Etain begins to experience as she nurtures a genuine warmth and fondness for the good King Eochy.

She also feels pity for the pathetic and weak desires of his brother, Ailill. Ailill also represents the darker side of Eochy's tender-heartedness. Often men who display strength, nobility and apparent gentleness, are stubbornly proud and are afraid of their weaker, Ailill side. They are afraid to acknowledge that they have feelings and often deny themselves access to their softer, more feminine side. Ailill represents that part of a man's psyche that unconsciously elects to revel in the torment of compulsive and obsessive desire rather than to reveal to himself that he actually has 'feelings'.

Etain has not yet met romance in her mortal life, but by her desire to help the weak Ailill she is putting herself into a far more dangerous position, not by her own apparent doing but by her fall from grace. This occurs in many stories that require the protagonist to 'grow' psychologically. Her mortal, compassionate nature takes pity on the dying Ailill, and she wants only to save him from his death. If she must do as he bids to save his life, she will be unfaithful in body, but will she be unfaithful in mind and heart also? Here is her chance to be transported to the woods to test her loyalty to the king. Will she make an error of human judgement and risk a fall from grace or is there some mysterious power at work that can save her? Fate intervenes, and Midhir returns unseen, casts a spell over the love-sick Ailill and takes his place in the woods as the wretched mortal. Etain is thus ironically freed from deceiving her husband, Eochy, for Midhir rejects her in his disguise as Ailill, recognizing that she is not 'in love' with this wretch of a man, only filled with deep human pity for him.

When Etain's choice really becomes manifest, when she has to choose between her love for Eochy and her desire for Midhir, she has no time to reflect. She promises Midhir she will be with him, but he must give her time to allow Eochy to come to terms with his loss. Her instinctual nature gives her the chance to tell the truth to her husband. But she doesn't. Why doesn't Etain reveal all to Eochy? Why does she ponder upon it for days and weeks? Is it for fear of hurting Eochy or is it for fear of losing the only man who can offer her the warmth and genuine goodness of human love? Intuitively, she does not discuss the matter with Eochy, but at the same time she betrays her love for Midhir. She can choose neither and by remaining silent, it is up to Midhir to return to claim her. Etain so far has learned that honour, respect, companionship and compassion are as essential to her growth as is romantic love. This is the power of woman. But she reacts from fear, rather than from genuine commitment to her marriage.

Etain still longs for something, the divine, for the spiritual to give her meaning in life. This is the light, or the flame, for which we all search and often find in passionate relationships. So when Midhir returns for her at a great feast, this time she does not hesitate to go. She must experience the wrenching apart, the suffering, the pain and the intensity of her desire to become truly aware of her self. Many of us, however, do not use these moments or these encounters to give us meaning or to re-connect us to what we may have lost.

Etain flies away with divine love, is transported to some magic place with Midhir, and she finds that it hurts. She has sacrificed the compassionate nature of her mortal king for the passionate flames of a divine god. Now she must suffer. But through the love of her king and the purpose of his search for her, Etain is given a second chance to return to human love.

Eochy calls upon Dalan's magical powers. To find Etain they burn bark to reveal the words of where she may be found. Symbolically, Eochy must allow his own passions, his own instincts, to burn through his heart to give him the strength and courage to set out and restore Etain to his side. Often men are too proud, too fearful of their feminine nature, to venture forth, but by allowing passion to well up from the unconscious and burn through his skin like the bark of the yew tree, Eochy is preparing himself for the final confrontation.

But it is Midhir, one of the immortal and all-seeing gods, who reluctantly understands the twisting of fate. He accepts that Eochy has as much right to Etain's love as he does. Etain must be returned to the king, but not without some insight first into her own heart. Eochy comes for his queen, and Midhir arranges for Eochy's test. But it is Etain who reveals to Eochy that she still loves him out of the fifty *doppelgängers* who walk beside her. She could have remained cold, indifferent, a mere puppet, but her love shines out through her sad eyes, for she feels deeply and knows that she is still human and must share human love. Her journey to reach this point has been long and filled with suffering, but then, so is every human journey. From the time before we are born and are all gods, all goddesses, until the time we must return to Erin as immortals again, in between we have to learn to accept our earthly boundaries as well as our divine yearnings. Perhaps it is through this very humanness that we can glimpse the soul from which we seem so disconnected.

For Etain a new awareness grows within. One day she will return to Erin and to Midhir. But for now human love is enough. Midhir will wait for her, as surely as Eochy came to find her.

Orpheus and Eurydice

Origins and Traditions

THE story of Orpheus's love for Eurydice shows how, even when the most apparently dark and painful experience comes into our lives, it can sometimes be a means to a better way forward.

As we noted in the Introduction, the ancient Greeks had specific ideas about love. The tragedy of erotic, transformative love is to be found throughout their great dramas, writings and poetry. Their myths are filled with secret liaisons, passionate deities and tortured mortals, who are forced into deeds that cause terrible pain, or souls torn apart by love and desire.

Greek mythology is probably the best-known aggregation of allegories and legends in the West. The Greek pantheon, perhaps more than that of any other mythology, is embedded deep within the Western psyche. We still find remnants of the jewels of the great goddess heritage of the Minoan and pre-Aryan patriarchal societies studded in the fabric of the male-dominated myths of ancient Greece. Yet although we may have forgotten how the world was before the great civilization that was Greece produced such extraordinarily powerful images, it is through its ancient mythology that we can begin to discover how the wheel turned and the balance of our psycho-spiritual harmony began to change course.

The deities and mortals portrayed represent the archetypal forces that live through every one of us. Their potency, their beauty and their weaknesses are representative of the energies that each individual manifests to a greater or lesser extent. Sometimes we fall desperately in physical love, as if Eros has surfaced to our consciousness, as if we can only do as he bids, as if there was a tidal wave of passion on which we somehow manage to surf.

This story is the classic Hellenic version, which was probably based on an earlier Thracian myth on to which the whole Orphic belief system was later attached. In the pre-Hellenic myth, Eurydice was the mother of fate and akin to Persephone in her dual aspect in the Underworld. In the Thracian version the snake that bit her was merely her companion, and early iconography of this story shows a serpent at her feet rather than a snake biting her. In the earlier version it was, in fact, Eurydice as goddess of the Underworld, accompanied by her serpent, who welcomed Orpheus's soul into the Underworld, and it was only the later, more commonly known, Hellenic myth that portrayed Eurydice as Orpheus's wife and lover.

In this particular myth Orpheus, like most of us, cannot let go of the past. This is a dilemma common to both women and men, for within us all is both the soul and the spirit, the yin and the yang, the *anima* and the *animus*, the male and the female. But when the one we love seems to carry all the opposite energy for us and when we lose that person, it can seem that we have also lost part of our self.

Learning to let go is one of the most difficult lessons we face in love and relationships, but it is only when we finally relinquish the pain that we can allow something or someone else to enter our lives and we can move on another step in our journey.

'Those who do not possess, have no fear of loss.'

The Myth

ORPHEUS was a poet and musician, and his beautiful songs and inspiring music made even the trees uproot themselves, boulders melt and rivers change their courses. The wild beasts of the forests and hills would listen as he drifted across the countryside, playing his lyre and reminding all that heard him of the eternal dance and music of nature.

Orpheus had been to Colchis with the Argonauts. His singing and music had kept the armies light-hearted, spirited and hopeful that they would return from their great battle. When Orpheus returned home, he married the nymph Eurydice, the woman of his dreams.

Aristaeus was the son of Apollo and the nymph Cyrene. He was also the cousin of Orpheus and had heard that Orpheus had recently married one of the most exquisite of all women. Aristaeus was a wanderer. He knew how to keep bees, to make cheese, to blend herbs and to grow olives. He travelled across Greece, teaching these skills to anyone he met, and one day as he strolled through the woods of Thessaly he came across Eurydice bathing in the River Peneus. Eurydice was naked and without doubt one of the loveliest nymphs he had ever seen. Aristaeus couldn't prevent his own sexual feelings from overwhelming him, and he threw himself into the river in an attempt to rape her. Eurydice escaped and ran up the riverbank in panic, but as she ran, she trod on a snake, which sank its fangs deep into her foot. Within minutes she was dead. When Eurydice's sisters heard that Aristaeus was responsible for her death, they punished him by killing all his bees.

When Orpheus heard the news of Eurydice's death he ran quickly to where she had supposedly fallen, but unknown to Orpheus, Hades had already taken her to the Underworld. Unable to accept the fact of Eurydice's death, Orpheus set off at once to find her alive or dead. He travelled across Greece searching for her, believing that her body had been taken from the riverbank and hidden in some dark cave. He played his lyre everywhere he went in the hope that she would hear him and come to him. But it was the god Hermes who finally took pity on Orpheus and told him that she had been taken to the Underworld.

Orpheus could not bear the finality of his beloved's death, and his grief turned to unbearable and wretched longing for her. In his torment, he set out to do what no man had ever done before. He boldly plunged into the dark tunnels and passageways that led to the Underworld. When he reached the River Styx he played his lyre and sang sweet music and songs to lull and seduce the ferryman, Charon, to take him across the river. When he met Cerberus, the three-headed dog who was the watchdog of the gate to the Underworld, he enchanted him to sleep with his music, as he did the three judges of the dead. In the heart of the darkness, at the deepest vortex of the Underworld, all hell's torments and pain momentarily ceased because of his beautiful music.

He was met by Persephone and Hades, who asked him to play to them. Not usually known for their benevolence, they allowed him to stay a while so that the dead were soothed, and all who heard him, including Eurydice, wept for the upper world. Orpheus's plaintive words and poignant music touched even Persephone and Hades, and they agreed to his pleas for them to release Eurydice back to the upper world.

'But there shall be one condition,' decided Hades. Orpheus put down his lyre and listened to the silence of the Underworld, knowing that he could do nothing but agree. If he could take Eurydice back to their happy and blissful existence, he would agree to anything.

'What is it that I must do?' he asked.

'It is not what you must do, it is what you must not do,' grinned the great lord of the darkness. Yet Orpheus could not see his face, for none but Persephone had ever gazed on Hades beneath his dark cloak.

'Then tell me quickly, for I would wish only to return my love to her life and to my heart.'

Hades rose from his great obsidian throne. He swept his great cloaks of darkness across the ground, past Orpheus and towards the tunnels of gloom where lingered the dead who had not yet arrived and those who had not yet departed.

'It is possible to leave the Underworld only if you do not look back.'

'I shall easily avoid turning my gaze back to the Underworld! Why should I want to look back upon the darkness on my way to the light?' replied Orpheus. How easy was this request, surely Hades did not think for one minute that he, Orpheus, a mortal, would ever want to look back!

'But that is not quite all.' Hades pulled his swirling cloak around him, and rocks tumbled down the sides of the great cavern as he turned suddenly, his powerful footsteps shaking the ground beneath him. 'For neither must you glance back at Eurydice. Not one look as she follows you, not one turn of the head, not one motion of your eye behind you. For to gaze upon the dead, to see her soul with your own mortal eye, can mean only one thing: that she will dissolve before you. Her loveliness will become a wretched memory, her beauty will be your darkness, never your light. To see a soul – for a mortal being ever to see a soul – is to condemn that soul to eternal death. Do you understand?'

Orpheus took a deep breath, he had no choice. 'I will do as you bid, sir. I will not look at Eurydice until I have reached the upper world.'

'Keep your eyes straight forwards. Look only to the upper world. Look only to those who come towards you, and then once you have passed into the land of light, you may then, and only then, turn to see your beloved.'

But Orpheus's agony was so intense, so wretchedly filling his mind and tormenting his soul, that the thought of not looking at Eurydice until they reached the light of the upper world began to tear him apart. What if Hades were playing a trick on him? What if this being that stepped so softly behind him was not Eurydice but some ghastly demon, which would follow him to the light to plague him and torture him about his true love? These thoughts spun in Orpheus's head. He could not trust his instincts but began to analyse and question his own doubts and wonder if he could believe the words of the guardian of the Underworld. Hades lived in a realm cloaked in darkness. Could his words be a masquerade, too? Could it be that Hades really wanted to keep Eurydice for himself?

Unable to trust his intuition, his imagination plagued him with fantasies, with strange images of his own doom as he returned to the upper world. There was nothing left within his mind or heart on which he could rely.

Hermes guided Orpheus back through the dark tunnels and dank caverns to the edges of the Underworld. A soft hand touched his from behind and then entwined his own fingers. But he dared not look round. The skin was cold, but it was mortal. Surely no demon could possess such velvet skin, surely no ghost or phantom could feel so real? As they walked further and further towards the light, Orpheus became more fearful that whoever it was that walked behind him and the soft hand that he held in the darkness was not that of Eurydice.

Orpheus's own mistrust and his own disbelief were his downfall. As they reached the very brink of the upper world, as the first chink of light sparkled through a crack in the rocky cavern, Orpheus could not resist looking back to see who it was that walked behind him – to make sure that it was Eurydice that he was taking back into life; to make sure that Hades had not tricked him.

As he turned round to look and saw her there for a second, he knew that he should have trusted himself, for at that moment, as they gazed into each other's eyes, Eurydice dissolved into thin air. Her image faded before him, a lonely face crying for his love, as it turned into darkness, the face that he had longed to kiss! Orpheus's hopes for happiness were

'Eurydice dissolved into thin air'

shattered. He could not believe what he had done. How could he have not trusted in himself? Where was Eurydice now?

'Eurydice! Eurydice! Come back! It is my mistake. I should not have turned round. I should have trusted you. I should have trusted myself!'

But no one came from the blackness to save him. The silence was more powerful than even his melodies. Orpheus sank down to the ground and wept. But he would not give in. For seven days and nights, overcome with grief and anger, he searched the tunnels of the Underworld, trying to convince himself he would find Eurydice again. But this time when he reached the River Styx the old ferryman, Charon, refused to ferry him across the river. His songs were no longer a fair price to pay his way. He blundered his way back up to the upper world like a man drunk on grief. In his misery, he had forgotten to drink the water of Lethe to obliterate all memory of the Underworld, and now Orpheus would never forget the terrible experiences of the Underworld or his love for Eurydice.

Orpheus went to live a hermit-like existence on Mount Peangaeum. He climbed to the peak each night, waiting to worship Apollo when the morning sun arose. His inner turmoil turned him against any kind of intimate relationship, and he especially refused the company of women. Many people heard that he had travelled to the Underworld and had returned to the upper world alive. Young men, in awe of his journey, came to hear his secrets of beyond the grave and to share in his worship of Apollo, the god of light. Some said he could find comfort only in the companionship of men, others that he had begun a strange cult that relied on his mysterious teachings of his journey to the Underworld and back.

Aristaeus meanwhile had wandered around the world, trying without success to find new swarms of bees. He still felt ridden with guilt for the part he had played in Eurydice's death, and one day, advised by his mother, the nymph Cyrene, he asked the old man of the sea, Proteus, how he could find any bees.

'You must sacrifice four bulls and four cows to the memory of Eurydice. This will cleanse your conscience. But do not burn the carcasses. You must leave them to rot.'

Aristaeus duly sacrificed the animals. But the memory of Eurydice lingered on, and after a few days the rotting carcasses filled only his senses with foul smells and guilty thoughts. Then, as he turned dejectedly back to searching for his bees, swarms of insects arose from the carcasses of the animals to fill his hives again.

Orpheus's worship of Apollo aroused the anger of Eurydice's fellow-nymphs. Some of these were the Maenads, the female worshippers of Dionysus, the god of ecstasy and wine. They came one night to the cave where Orpheus was teaching his disciples and took the knives and weapons left at the entrance to the cave. In their anger and madness, they hacked Orpheus to pieces and threw the parts of his body into the sea, nailed his head to his lyre and tossed it into the River Hebrus. But the lyre and the head floated downstream without sinking, still singing and playing plaintive songs, calling for Eurydice wherever it went. The head floated out to sea, and when it arrived at Lesbos the islanders buried the head in the temple to appease Dionysus's rage, and Apollo hung the lyre in the sky as one of the constellations.

Orpheus's death meant that he could be reunited with Eurydice in the Underworld, and they could gaze into each other's eyes as they could not do when Orpheus was chained to his life in the upper world, and she to hers below.

Reflections

The essential quality of this story revolves around the apparent bliss that Orpheus enjoys and that we might all experience when in the throes of 'true love'. Married to the woman of his dreams, Orpheus is set for a happy-ever-after ending, but what seems to be a tale of great joy and happiness turns to a terrible tragedy. Orpheus has to learn about love and about himself on two levels. The first is to learn to accept the ending of his relationship, which he is unable to do. He denies the finality of Eurydice's death and believes that he can turn back the clock and that he, unlike all others, can make things be the way they were before. This is common in our own lives. When a tragedy occurs, when a lover leaves us or falls out of love with us, we are convinced of our power to change things and to restore them to how they were before 'fate' changed and wrecked our lives. But what Orpheus does not realize, and what we as individuals often refuse to accept, is that we cannot go backwards, we cannot travel through time and be who we were before. We can only be who we are now.

Orpheus's world has crumbled. His lover has tragically died and because he cannot face this, he will not sacrifice this part of himself. We often have to make sacrifices and honour the giving up of something before we can move on in life. But Orpheus refuses to let go of Eurydice, or the mother of fate. If he can find the mother of fate he will control his own destiny again. When Eurydice is taken from him Orpheus feels as if he is being dissolved. The irony is that it is Eurydice's own dissolution later on, just at the moment he believes he has redeemed himself, that leads to his greatest sacrifice.

61

Orpheus must also face the fact that he has chosen his own path in life, no matter how much Eurydice or fate seems to play a part in it. He is his own fate, and every choice he makes in life means he must take responsibility for his own transformation.

When the usually gentle Aristaeus attacks Eurydice, we see how any of us can be overcome by sexual temptation. Yet it is, ironically, Aristaeus, not Orpheus, who achieves redemption. Aristaeus is overcome with remorse, but his bees are destroyed by Eurydice's sisters. Bees represent our thoughts, the busy workings of the mind, and it is as if the guilt and emotional reaction to what he has done prevent Aristaeus from being able to work, to think, to behave logic- ally. His bees – his rational and logical mind – have been destroyed by guilt. The only way to redeem himself is to make a sacrifice. This Aristaeus knows, but Orpheus does not. Both men make sacrifices, but their sacrifices are different.

The word sacrifice means 'to make sacred', to give up something to the divine. Aristaeus kills cattle, a fairly common ritual, and through this act, a sac- rifice to Eurydice's memory, he is redeemed. The bees rise from the rotting car- casses that held Eurydice's memory, and as the feelings and the guilt gradually turn to putrefied flesh, so arise his thoughts again, and so begins a change in Aristaeus's whole self. He has overcome the pain, and he is allowed to return to his bees and to his rational self, exactly because he has given something of himself to the gods. In other words, he has given up honourably – or sacrificed – the 'rotten' guilty feelings and memories of Eurydice.

But Orpheus has yet to sacrifice himself, for this is the only way he can ever let go. In the Underworld he persuades Hades and Persephone to let Eurydice return with him. There are times when we have no choice but to plunge into our own unconscious, our own 'underworld', to persuade our demons to allow us to be who we were before our loss. But it is these very gods and goddesses within who know that we cannot go back and re-create the past. For any crisis, any moment of awakening means we cannot return to what we were before. Crisis comes from a Greek word meaning 'turning point', to make a decision, to move forward.

So Orpheus is set a test. He has pleaded, he has enchanted and he has stirred compassion and sympathy in the hearts of the gods, but he cannot have his desire unless he can pass a test. The test that Hades sets him is to see if Orpheus will turn his head to look back at the one he loves. In fact, Orpheus has already done just that by trying to turn the present into the past and to recapture the few moments that he shared with Eurydice. Yet what were those moments? Was their love a deep friendship, perhaps a devoted love based on *agape*. Was it erotic love? Or was it a fragile and unstable relationship, built on 'being in love'? Could it be that Orpheus's projection of self had vanished along with Eurydice, and he now desperately wanted it back?

When we fall in love and the 'other' with whom we fall changes or moves on to someone new, we often demand to re-create the past. We cannot be left stranded in the same place alone, we cannot 'live without that person' and we would rather die than they not be at our side. This is the moment when we face the possibility that we may lose our own projection of our self, and it is painful because it is like losing part of ourselves, because it is exactly the reflection of ourselves that is lost.

So Orpheus wants his reflection back at all costs, and he will plunge into the realm of Hades and fight the demons or shadows lurking within the Underworld to find it. But Orpheus cannot resist looking back. Whether he truly doubts his own judgement that the silent ghost behind him is Eurydice or whether he is simply tempted to gaze on her beauty, he breaks his promise. And at the moment of breaking his promise, he loses all. Now he has no choice but to accept the inevitability of her death. There is no turning back. In a sense, when we spend so much time trying to fight the rejection or loss of a lover or partner, we are denying ourselves the chance to move on, to surrender ourselves to pain and allow the process to transform us on a deeper level.

Orpheus retreats to a rather ascetic type of existence, a common means of avoiding pain. He rejects women and turns to men for company, whether in friendship or sexually is irrelevant. He finds comfort in the worship of Apollo, but his inner journey, his trip to the Underworld and back, becomes attractive to outsiders. Young men hear of his exploits and, finding such heroic actions attractive, begin to join him in his cave, sharing in his stories and his cultish worship of Apollo. To have lived through such a tragedy, to have been down into the darkest recesses of the Underworld and to have come back alive is enviable. But Orpheus has still made no sacrifice. On the surface he may have given up a rich and glamorous lifestyle, he may have changed his habits and his diet, his worship and his friends, but underneath he has not given up anything, especially not the binding, possessive attachment to the loss of Eurydice. It is only the intervention and frenzied desire of the Maenads that allow Orpheus to find redemption. He must be sacrificed, whether by the worshippers of Dionysus or by his own hands. Ironically, by his physical death, his transformation takes place, both literally and on a psychological level. He can now be united with Eurydice in the Underworld. Now that he has finally let go of her memory, now that he has finally given up a part of himself, he can at last find inner reconciliation.

Nantu and Etsa

Origins and Traditions

SOUTH American mythology has been largely tainted by the arrival of Christianity and European settlement. Most myths carried on an oral tradition, concentrating on the generations of gods and their epic battles, crises and conflicts. These myths are often chaotic, filled with barbaric acts, sex, death and punishment. Little attention is paid to love, for what was love to early tribal peoples, whose life depended on both the rivalry between tribes and the struggle of living in the harsh conditions of weather and jungle?

There is little time for intellectual idealization to become conscious in the mythology of these highly complex peoples. The Jivaro of Ecuador were agriculturists but also aggressive warring people. Originally head-hunters, the Jivaro believed that they obtained their power against the fearsome spirits of their ancestors by shrinking the heads of their victims.

The story of Nantu and Etsa is taken from only a small part of a great epic tale of murder, lust and incest, but it reveals the powerful influence of the sun and moon and how closely the cycles of both these celestial bodies were followed in the daily lives of the Jivaro. As a love story, it carries the poignancy of unrequited love, but the unlucky victim of this suffering was not a god, a goddess or even a mortal, but a simple and much misunderstood creature, the goatsucker bird.

64

The Myth

ETSA was the son of Kumpara the Creator, and Etsa was the sun itself. So that Etsa could have a wife who would be unrelated to him, Kumpara had to devise a way to create her differently. So Kumpara took a handful of mud from the moist earth, placed it in Etsa's mouth when he was sleeping and blew a warm breath across Etsa's face. The lump of mud was transformed into Kumpara's daughter, Nantu, the moon.

Nantu's beauty was compelling to all who saw her. Each night, when the moon appeared ghostly silver in the sky, a great bird, the goatsucker, became infatuated with her magical presence. Many times he attempted to seduce her, but Nantu was not interested nor would she let him come near her in her heavenly chamber.

After many years Etsa the sun also fell in love with the exquisite Nantu, following her about the sky to demonstrate his love and affection for her. But Nantu was shy and would not let him come close too soon. Etsa found some herbal dye and painted his face to make him even more attractive than his usual radiant self. Nantu took this opportunity to escape from his passionate heart and disappeared by shooting up into the higher canopies of the sky. In her heavenly chamber she painted herself black with sua so that her body was the night. She also painted her face so that even now, you can see the strange faint markings on the surface of the moon. She climbed like a mountain jaguar up a steep trail into the sky and across the curving canopy of stars, there to hide from the sun and his seemingly lustful glow.

The goatsucker bird, Auhu, saw Nantu perilously high in the sky and, realizing that she was probably escaping from the demands of Etsa, decided to try his own luck at wooing her. A thick vine hung down from the sky's mantel, and the bird began to climb up towards the path that Nantu had taken in the night. When Nantu saw the bird cooing and billing his way up the vine, she cut through the thick woody stem. The great vine fell back into the jungle and ever since has tangled up all the jungles of the world. Auhu, the goatsucker, fell with it, and finding himself back on the earth, went to sulk in the trees.

Etsa was furious that Nantu had escaped from his advances again and decided to chase after her. The only way he could reach the sky was to fly, so he caught two parrots and two parakeets and tied them to his wrists and his knees. The birds flew up towards the moon where he finally met Nantu and demanded that she love only him. But Etsa's demands made Nantu more resolved to go her own way, and a terrible quarrel began. The quarrel turned to a fight, and Etsa, full of rage, struck Nantu. This was the first eclipse of the moon. Nantu was strong and fought back and in turn she hit Etsa across the belly. This was the first eclipse of the sun.

Nantu was exhausted by the passionate antics of the sun, and she began to weep. Etsa said: 'See how much stronger and more powerful I am, and you can only cry.' Now, whenever the face of the moon is red, it means that it is going to weep rain across the land.

Believing she had no choice, Nantu agreed to marry Etsa. Their first child was born by the River Kanusa. This was Unushi, the sloth, the first Jivaro.

The sun and moon often meet on earth. They leave the sky for a few nights, and then there is no moonlight. This is the time when they procreate. All the children of Etsa and Nantu are born on earth, and the waxing moon indicates the pregnancy, while the waning moon is the giving of birth. So the earth was used as a place for all their children to inhabit. Unushi, the sloth, the first Jivaro, was put in the forests, which became his home.

One day Nantu returned to earth to sort out a family quarrel. The enraged relative beat Nantu violently, threw her into a deep pit and covered her with earth. A dove witnessed what had happened and told his old friend, Auhu the goatsucker, about Nantu's terrible fate. Auhu now had another chance to show Nantu how much he loved her and to prove how worthy of her love he was. He adorned his face with colour and put on his beautiful beetle-wing earrings. Using a snail-shell as a trumpet, he began to blow through the instrument as he walked towards the pit, knowing that the vibrations would shake the soil loose from the earthy grave and allow Nantu to escape from the dark hole. But the shrill sound was so startling that as soon as the soil began to loosen, Nantu burst out of the hole and flew straight back up to the sky without even seeing Auhu in all his finery. Auhu called after her, 'Come back, come back!' but it was too late. Nantu did not look back.

So with his love unrequited, Auhu went back to his melancholy lifestyle. This is why on moonlit nights you can hear his mournful song that he cries to Nantu: 'Aishiru, Aishiru. Beloved, beloved.'

Reflections

As in so much South American mythology, the two divine principles are here in turmoil. The moon and the sun represent female and male, yin and yang, and in order for the world to be in balance they must unite in their heavenly chamber. However, in this particular story the moon, Nantu, has no interest in her divine consort, however much he decorates his face and adorns himself with jewels.

Self-beautification was an essential component in the rituals of the Jivaro and thus also became an integral part of their mythology. Nantu, the moon, also paints her body black to become the night itself, and her face still carries the strange markings we see when the moon is full. The symbolism as she escapes from the lustful glow of the sun setting below the horizon is enchanting. This is divine desire at its most celestial. This story also provides the Jivaro with an explanation for the eclipses of the sun and moon, a phenomenon that many civilizations have tried to explain. The eventual union of sun and moon, when they appear to come down to earth – that is, just before a new moon – produces all the inhabitants of earth and again demystifies the waxing and waning cycle of the moon.

Then comes the sad goatsucker, a bird of the night and a creature from earth to cause trouble. The goatsucker, which is also known as the nightjar and has been wrongly accused throughout the world of sucking the blood of goats. The goatsucker makes a re-appearance in an attempt to save Nantu from being buried alive. He dons his beetle-wing earrings and finds a snail-shell trumpet to call and awaken the moon from her suffocating chamber beneath the earth. This is the sadness of unrequited love, for not only does Nantu rapidly ascend back to her heavenly path when she is forced out of the ground by the magical call but she does not respond to him. The sad song of the goatsucker is heard across the land on moonlit nights, still calling for Nantu. We have all felt the emotion of loss, but none so great as the goatsucker's.

The Jivaro must have wondered how such a deity as the moon had not noticed the bird adorned in all his glorious finery. To these people, splendour and beauty were the magical ingredients of attraction to compensate for the lack of tenderness and compassion in their violent lives.

Idas and Marpessa

Origins and Traditions

THE story of Idas and Marpessa is one of the lesser known love stories of Greek mythology, and it portrays a different kind of love from many of the more passionate tales of unrequited love, tragic marriages and impossible triangles. Like much of Greek mythology, however, the complications of family inheritance, the twists and turns of relationships between father-in-laws, daughters, gods and cousins brings with it its own dark secrets and irony of plot.

Idas and Marpessa are both mortal (although between them they share a varied and divine ancestry), and their love is mortal, human and earthy. Certainly there is romance and they fall in love as do any other couple, but the tale reveals the way choices are often made through wisdom, knowledge, foresight and intuition rather than on impulse or because of status. This is the tale of a beautiful woman's choice, and yet it is also, ironically, the story of how our choices, our decisions, are truly also the weaving of our own fate. The Greeks believed that the Moirae wove our fate, but yet at the moment of making a choice it is the actual thread we hold out towards the Moirae that also determines the destiny that is woven for us.

The background of Idas and Marpessa is like the backdrop of a richly painted stage-set and is, in this instance, essential to the story as it unfolds.

The Myth

MARPESSA'S mother was Alcippe, the sister of the beautiful Hippodameia. Alcippe was no doubt present when their father, the anxiety-ridden Oenomaus, insisted that all Hippodameia's suitors must undergo a contest for her hand. Oenomaus seemed to be obsessed with oracles. He had once been told that if Hippodameia should ever marry he would die, and he therefore decided to make sure that she never did. Oenamaus was also king of Pisa and the son of Ares, just to make his lineage even more dramatic.

The beautiful Hippodameia was desired by every mortal far and wide so, rather ominously, Oenomaus set a trap for each suitor by challenging them to a chariot race that he knew he would win. The wretched suitors would win Hippodameia if they won the race, but lose their heads if they lost. Oenomaus always won because he ensured that his horses, his chariot and his charioteer were the fastest and the best. They also knew the route backwards. The heads of the challengers for his daughter's hand in marriage and of his rather gory sport were hung around the entrance to the palace gates.

It was in this strange and grisly obsession of Oenomaus's that the young Alcippe took great interest. Stories abounded about Oenomaus, including one that said that there were, in fact, no oracles about his fate and that he was desperately in love with his own daughter Hippodameia, taking great morbid delight in killing all the young men who came to court her.

Later on, Alcippe married Euenus, who was, like her father, a son of Ares. She no doubt mentioned the goings-on at the palace in Pisa, and the rather self-absorbed and neurotic Euenus caught on to the grim idea and decided to do exactly what his father-in-law had done – that is, contest any potential suitors for their own daughter, Marpessa. No doubt the sons of Ares were carriers of some rather unpleasant psychological family complexes that developed their fixation for this morbid sport. The god Ares, after all, was on the whole a rather brainless, unfeeling oaf, who raped and roared around the heavens like a spoilt child. Some sources even say he was only the child of Hera, and as such a mere manifestation of her own unresolved anger. However, Euenus never got very far with his own obsession for baiting young men, and this is where the story of Idas and Marpessa begins.

Some say that Marpessa's beauty enchanted many of the gods, but it was Apollo who saw her first, and from the moment he saw her was bewitched by her grace and the music of her voice. Each day Apollo, the sun-god, drove his chariot across the sky, and as he neared the sea he saw beneath him two beings walking upon the sand, their faces close, their eyes upon each other only. This was Marpessa and the youth Idas. And from that moment Apollo desired only to have this beautiful woman, Marpessa, in body and in soul.

Marpessa had not known Idas for long, but she had found him to be like a friend, a mortal with gentle hands. A young man, full of life and charm, he made her laugh, made her smile and mostly made her feel as if there was only joy in the world.

Idas had been in love with Marpessa for many months, and yet always there was the terrible memory of his first meeting with Marpessa's father, Euenus. He had come to the king's palace to ask if he might marry Marpessa, but Euenus was cold, unfeeling and opposed to his cherished daughter marrying such a youth, with no status and no wealth and nothing to offer her except love. Euenus ordered him from the palace, for he could not even consider the match, let alone lower himself to challenge the boy to a chariot race for her hand. He had heard the stories of Alcippe's father, a powerful and evil man, who had challenged every suitor for her sister to take part in a chariot race. If the suitor lost, he would die. Many heroes, many mortals, had braved the test, and all had failed. Alcippe had described in gruesome detail the heads that hung around her father's house as a grim reminder of Oenomaus's own cunning powers. Euenus himself was also fond of such blood-thirsty sport and had toyed with the same idea for Marpessa's suitors. Perhaps a different kind of death was the answer for the loser of the race, but few came to test their skills as a charioteer. No doubt, thought Euenus, none was good enough to take his daughter from him. Euenus, like his father, the god Ares, was passionate about his own offspring.

It was with heavy heart that Idas left the palace that day. But his unworthiness was perhaps what saved him, for if he had been challenged to the chariot race, he would surely have lost Marpessa, if not his head. Marpessa went quickly to her father's chamber when she heard that Idas's proposal had been rejected. She swept her hand across the marble table, impatient as her father dressed, bathed and prepared himself for her visit.

He came before her dressed in purple robes, like a great god himself, like the images of Zeus that played in her head. But no, her father was not a god, only descended from a god whose only interest was in the stirrings of his own loins. So Marpessa smiled sweetly at her forbidding father. His brow was wet from his bath, yet she knew his resolve would never weaken.

'Euenus, dear father,' pleaded Marpessa, 'why can you not reconsider?'

'Because Idas is not worthy of you, child. You must only marry someone with power and wisdom, perhaps a god may come for you. Hah! Yet even a god must be challenged to a chariot race. For unless they can beat my own chariots of gold, they are not worthy of you, not even the gods. You are descended from the gods, and only to the gods may you give your heart!'

Marpessa was saddened by her father's obsession with the gods and his refusal to listen to her. She wandered hopelessly down to the seashore, for she knew Idas waited there to hear her news.

The boy sat alone, watching Apollo's golden chariot reach the highest point of the heavens. His love for Marpessa seemed impossible. She had not rejected him, she had not even said she loved him yet, but he knew deep in his heart that she did. For a woman to be fathered by such a man as Euenus gave him great doubts and fears about Marpessa's own sanity. Yet he loved her, there was nothing he could do about it, except believe in that love.

She came towards him, running through the meadows, pulling strands of grass from their sheaths in anger and sadness. She stopped beside him and whispered. 'No, he has said no. Our marriage cannot be, Idas.'

He turned his sad eyes to her and nodded. 'I will always love you, Marpessa, and somehow, one day we shall be together, I know it in my heart.'

Then he stood, took Marpessa's hand and kissed her lips, as if for the last time. She watched him walk towards the sea, and then, falling on his knees, he held out his arms to the great ocean and with one mournful cry for help from Poseidon, he washed the tears from his face with the salt and the foam of the waves as they crashed against his body.

But while the lovers had been secretly meeting, Apollo had driven his chariot of gold to the palace to visit Euenus. He had seen the unhappiness of the lovers and knew that time was precious if he were to have Marpessa for himself. This wondrous jewel was to be his at all costs, whatever the price. For he was the god Apollo, a prophet and a bringer of light. And now with his usual impulses stirred and his unforgiving frame of mind set, he drove fast to Euenus to be sure that he made Marpessa his before any other god.

Euenus was most pleased to receive the great Apollo in his palace, and he listened eagerly and greedily to Apollo's desire. How fortunate that a great god like Apollo should honour him by marrying his daughter!

How ridiculous and insignificant the youth Idas now seemed!

'Indeed, I would that you do me the honour of taking my daughter's hand. But even a god must prove himself worthy,' said the devious Euenus.

'How, in what manner am I to be tested by a king? I am a magnificent god, and there is nothing that I cannot do! My desire for your daughter is so powerful that you can challenge me if you will, but I am surely the victor.' Apollo smiled, certain of his victory, certain of his power.

'All the suitors for Marpessa's hand must undergo this test, you must understand. But it is simple. We shall race our chariots, and if you win, then surely you can marry Marpessa.' Apollo nodded and shrugged his shoulders. Let the older man have his fun. There would be little doubt that Apollo would win, especially as Euenus wanted his daughter to wed the god.

Idas had spent the afternoon on the seashore, praying to Poseidon for help. He called across the ocean, asking only that he be given a winged chariot so that he might fly away with Marpessa to a place where her father could never find her. Eventually, Poseidon agreed and sent across the sea a wonderful chariot, silver winged and filled with jewels.

Marpessa sat alone beside the stone fountain, watching the great Apollo prepare for the chariot race. His was, indeed, the most beautiful face she had seen, and he was wise, noble and proud. A great god who really loved her. How easy it would be to live with Apollo in his kingdom. How fine and exquisite would be his palace, and how generous and fulfilling would be his love. He came across to her and gazed at her lovely face, then placed his golden hands against her soft skin.

Marpessa could not speak, for she thought only of Idas and his sweet gentle love. This god, his greatness, his fire, his passion – were they truly what she wanted? But before she could answer, before she could place her finger upon his great golden hand to tell him, there came the thundering of storm clouds from the seashore. Marpessa turned to look, and gasped, for it was not a storm, with rolling clouds churning on the wind, but a winged chariot, charging towards her, and Idas laughing, holding the reins and shouting to her to come.

'Come to me now, Marpessa! Before it is too late! Take hold of my hand and ride away from this land forever!'

Without hesitating she grasped his hand as he snatched her into the air, his strength astounding now that he was ahead. Apollo's smiling face turned suddenly to fierce anger and desire, for the mortal had stolen his one and only love.

But it was Euenus who moved first. Possessed with jealousy, he jumped into his own chariot and, like a man ablaze with hatred, surged his horses onwards after the silver chariot that carried Marpessa away. Idas drove faster and faster, until the landscape became blurred with colour, and the sea and the sky became a haze of blue against Marpessa's flowing hair.

'He's catching up. He is filled with rage and fury! I am scared, Idas, so fearful of his wrath!' screamed Marpessa, but Idas merely drove on like a man possessed by a power that was not his own, as if Poseidon himself burst forth across the land. Soon, Euenus's horses began to tire, and Euenus himself began to realize that he would never catch the magnificent winged chariot. His pursuit was in vain, and his anger turned to despair. He saw ahead of him the great River Lycormas, which he knew would be impossible to cross now. But this wild, untamed and treacherous side of Euenus, the rage that he had inherited from his father Ares, turned inwards on himself. In a moment of deep and dark hopelessness, he threw himself into the raging waters of the great river. The dark muddy waters closed over his head, and Euenus was gone. From that day the river has been called the River Euenus.

Idas and Marpessa swept on, unaware of the plight of the king, but knowing now that someone else was surely following. The jealous and enraged sun-god had begun to catch up in his own golden chariot as it crossed the sky. Nearer and nearer Apollo lurched his mighty chariot, until Idas was sure they would be struck down with lightning and fire. Idas quickly halted his chariot, and Marpessa jumped out on to the land, to find Apollo before her. She grasped Idas by the arm, but Apollo smiled. He knew that he was now the victor, and that Idas would have to die.

But as the mortals trembled with fear, the great Zeus spoke from the heavens. Thunderbolts shook the mountainsides, and the earth trembled at his voice. Apollo looked up to the skies and let go of Marpessa's arm, for he would have seized her there and then.

'Let her decide!' boomed the great voice. It was enough for Apollo to release his hold and only gaze in wonder at her beauty again. And she, entranced by his own exquisite face, could only listen to the words he spoke. He held out a fragile flower to her, plucked from the bank beside the meadow. His golden face and his silken desire were drawing her to him. The velvet music that came from between his lips sang more than mortal love to her as he implored her to choose only he, the great Apollo.

'Listen to me, Marpessa. You are a mortal, but I can give you immortality. Here on earth you will grow old, your beauty will fade and you will die, but come with me and I will make you as immortal as I! In the heavens is no unhappiness, no despair, no sorrow. You can never know such love as the love of a god. It is beyond mortal love, and the desire I feel for you is all for you and for none other.'

Then Marpessa turned to Idas, whose face was white and who was numb with fear. Tired and silent, he cast his eyes down, away from the radiance of the sun-god's face.

'And Idas, what do you say?'

'What can I say when such dreams can be yours? How can I inspire you to love like this god, when I am only a mortal? I can make no promises but offer only the love of a human being. You are a woman. I cannot persuade you otherwise, for you are the mystery that shines out of my soul. For that I love you, and for that I would die.'

Idas turned then, and gazed back towards the sea. Now he was silent, his love could not be more perfect than his words. So they stood there awhile, this god, this woman and this man. Marpessa looked upon the two who loved her, her heart searching for the answer. And then at last, after what seemed a silence of eternity but was only perhaps a minute, Marpessa spoke, first to Apollo.

'To share the gift of immortality is perhaps the most treasured desire in life. What more could I ask? What more could any woman want? To be the wife of a great god and to have everything in the world must be every woman's dream. But in a world of paradise, there may be something missing for me, for I have known pain, I have known what it is to feel tears upon my cheek. I am only human, however eternal I may become. And if you give me immortality, you cannot give me eternal youth. For I shall wither and grow ugly, my beauty will die, and you, you will stay forever young, forever golden and shining like the sun itself. How can I or you live with that?'

She turned to Idas then, and yet still he bowed his head, unsure of her final judgement. 'But if I marry Idas, then I shall find human love. Companionship and friendship that is true compassion. We shall grow old together, he and I. We shall both share the pain of mortality, but I shall not be abandoned because I am no longer beautiful, for that is what I fear if I were to wed a great god.'

Apollo frowned. He could not bear to hear her words. Was she teasing them? Was she only playing with this youth and testing his own magnificent power? He reached out his hands to touch her, but she shook her head. 'No, it cannot be, Apollo. For as much as I love you, you will remember me one day when we are old, and you will remember that once I was young and beautiful and that you loved me. For I must stay with Idas.'

Apollo's rejection was spoken. And as Idas took Marpessa's hand and they climbed into the winged chariot, a darkness fell across the earth. That night there was no sunset, for Apollo in his anger and sadness had hidden far away in the heavens, so that only darkness clothed the earth. But Idas and Marpessa were at last together, and their love grew into a deep and binding one, which no god could pull apart.

For many years Idas and Marpessa lived happily. It seems that Marpessa had only one child, Alcyone (usually known as Cleopatra), but the subsequent history of the family appears to have been Marpessa's ironic fate. Not only was her father already dead, but her son-in-law, Meleager, died, her daughter hanged herself, and eventually Idas was killed in a family quarrel with his old rivals, the heavenly twins, Castor and Polydeuces. Marpessa was left alone, abandoned and old, exactly what she had feared happening to her if she had married Apollo.

Reflections

Marpessa's love for Idas is not a mysterious, divine, magical ideal, but a human, earthy love for another being. It would have been easy for Marpessa to fall in love with Apollo and to be swept off her feet by the promise of divine love. She is infatuated with Apollo – after all, who could resist such a charmer? – but eventually her deeper womanly intuition guides her to make a choice in her own best interests.

Apollo is a notoriously glamorous and lustful god, who has made his way through numerous affairs with nymphs and goddesses. In our own lives we often meet the same type of figure – brash, handsome, good-looking and beautiful. Such men and women are often detached from their feelings, but they are people who seem to radiate a solar quality that is self-possessed and invincible. Marpessa herself is known for her extraordinary beauty and obviously attracts any man. Her background is unusual, for the male side of her family is riddled with obsessive, power-tripping, egotistical and incestuous men. She stands apart from the family curse, for Marpessa embodies the softer, receptive nature of yin energy, the side that has a closer connection to the natural rhythms, the laws of nature, as opposed to the laws of ego.

Idas is a youth with a simple desire, one that we have perhaps all experienced. He has fallen desperately in love with Marpessa and wants to contain and maintain the ideal image he has projected on to her through marriage. Strangely enough, Apollo wants to experience this too, but Apollo's love is divinely driven, and because he is a god he cannot enter fully into human suffering and despair. Idas represents those qualities in each of us when we fall in love – moments of ecstasy tinged with moments of pain. Apollo, on the other hand, is a god. He cannot suffer, he cannot feel pain. He has twinges of jealousy only because a god never comes second best. But Apollo is also divine, and his love is inhuman. He cannot offer Marpessa any of those empathetic qualities that she so desperately clings to for her survival.

The story centres on Marpessa's choice of mortal or god. Unlike many other love stories, this myth reminds us that all we can be is human. To dally with the gods can seem like a chance to experience divine or spiritual love for ever. But the dalliance can also illuminate our mortal fleshy selves, delimiting for us the truth that divine encounters, or spiritual enlightenment, can be an obsessive cradle into which we easily fall and out of which we then dare not venture. Our path to knowing ourselves better, of plunging into our unconscious and coming back with answers, is then blocked. To remain attached only to the numinous, to be cocooned by religious escapism or to be smothered by spiritual veils, is to deny our earthly connection. Our feet must walk upon the ground. Marpessa honours this human-ness, but only after she has experienced an encounter with a real god and come back to earth with a bump. The distortion of the inner world can be as illusory as the hall of mirrors that is our outer one.

Apollo was famous for his oracular vision. But this vision was deliberately ambiguous, and that is exactly the enigma of an oracle. An oracle offers an insight into a situation, a direction and a method of choice by offering mysterious, yet intuitive wisdom. Apollo could not foresee the future, otherwise he would certainly not have bothered even to enter the race for Marpessa. His watchword, 'Know thyself', was engraved above the stone shrine at Delphi. It is perhaps indicative in this story that Apollo also symbolizes the process that came to Marpessa to truly know *her*self.

Apollo plays two roles in Marpessa's choice – the oracular wisdom or the trigger to 'know herself', and the pure solar principle that urges us on in life and gives us purpose, whether we are female or male. This solar light inspires us and gives us a spark to illuminate our way. Marpessa's ancestry is full of solar men. In some ways we must face our solar nature, our purposeful ego and acknowledge this 'god' before we can truly 'love' another person. Marpessa does this: she faces Apollo and knows that prestige, 'immortality' and money could all be hers. But is that what she truly wants? She has begun a process in which she must make a choice, but then Idas charges along in his winged chariot and the decision is temporarily postponed.

The winged chariot given by Poseidon represents the mysterious numinous force that carries us all beyond our everyday reality. Poseidon is the god of the oceans, the essence of the time before we were born when we were at 'one' with the universe. The unknown realms of the deepest parts of the ocean where Poseidon lives are as murky and impenetrable as our own blank past, the time that stretches infinitely backwards before we were born. Poseidon's gift to Idas (and we do not know why he agreed to help Idas), suggests that both Idas and Marpessa must make a journey in this hazy, dreamlike state of dissolution before they can actually get on with the practicalities of love. As individuals, we must sometimes enjoy a ride on the winged chariot and allow it to transport us temporarily away from the world we consider to be 'real', to enjoy a pause in the machinery of life as we sample the best claret in Poseidon's cellars. In other words, sacred timelessness can be balanced with the profane, as long as we are aware we are doing so. To choose the path of eternal bliss above all else, however, can be dangerous if our feet are not placed squarely on the ground at the end of the chariot's journey.

But the winged chariot seems able to beat even Euenus at his obsessive and neurotic race. The implications of this are tremendous. In a sense, because Marpessa and Idas are experiencing such powerful forces in the winged chariot of love, they can perhaps now overcome the family curse. Euenus cannot keep up with them and is not powerful enough to destroy their bond, so in the end he can only destroy himself. The archetype of Euenus appears in contemporary families in a subtle, more diffuse disguise. Although Euenus may not have collected quite as many young men's heads around his front door as his father-in-law Oenomaus, he delights in the sacrifice of suitors for his daughter's hand. This is Euenus at his worst. This is Euenus making sacrifices in the form of other men's lives. There are many parents who unconsciously would make a similar sacrifice of their potential daughters- or sons-in-law. How often do we hear the words: 'How dare you choose someone I don't approve of? How could you go out with him or her? You are too young to marry. You are better than him or her. He or she not good enough for you.' Family members may not literally kill our prospective partners and they may not challenge them to chariot races, but they often believe they have some divine right to make decisions for us. Some do it with honour and grace, and acknowledge it as such. But there are many who are more likely to bear unconscious resentment, despising their children's inability to live up to 'family' expectations or, as it may be, narrow-minded values. Euenus is such a man, but he loses Marpessa, and his own life, because he represents the worst form of hubris – that of judgement.

Euenus's drowning also symbolizes a different level of awareness. Robert Graves, in his learned and brilliant interpretation of the Greek myths, suggests that in fact the drowning of Euenus has been misinterpreted and it is Idas himself who enters the river to purify himself before his marriage to Marpessa. Could this also imply that Euenus is another aspect of Idas, the dark face that all of us share? This is when we must remember that Apollo is still out there, with divine power on his side. It is not enough to escape in a chariot of dreams or to throw oneself into the river of life in order to avoid the truth. Idas must face Apollo as we must face our solar conscience. It is his only chance for real commitment with Marpessa.

With the death of Euenus, Marpessa and Idas have to face the wisdom and divinity of Apollo. Marpessa has taken the chariot ride, found out about sublime and sacred love, fallen into the chasm of physical bliss, but now has to face reality and the possibility that divine desire has more power than human value. But Marpessa seems to have grown in awareness since her chariot ride. She has discovered that there is more to love than passion – that human love and human life are also about compassion. Apollo knows none of these, for he is a god. He has no human feelings. Marpessa also knows she is beautiful, but like the flower that lasts only one day, she deliberates on the fact that her own beauty cannot last either.

Apollo could well have taken her back to Olympus there and then. Marpessa would have had no choice if Apollo had killed Idas. But Marpessa is offered a choice by the intervention of Zeus, who simply says, 'Let her decide!'

Marpessa has learned about intuitive wisdom. She has discovered that her solar, dynamic energy functions well alongside her feminine nature. But the choice is still hard, like any major choice in life.

So Apollo puts forward his case. He can offer Marpessa immortality and the wonders of Olympus. She cannot deny her passion for him, her powerful desire for this beautiful god is certainly disturbing, but yet there seems to be something wrong. She turns to Idas, and suddenly, seeing him downcast and hopeless, is filled with something stronger. Compassion. Empathy fills her heart, and she warms to the human-ness of Idas. Whether she truly loves him with an intense erotic passion is never made clear, but she has taken a trip in the winged chariot with him, and she has come back to earth with a bump.

Marpessa reveals her choice to both. Based on her fear of abandonment, of losing her beauty in old age and Apollo's own record for dumping his lovers, she chooses the sensible, earthy Idas. Friendship, companionship is enough. She has bitten into the apple and fallen into the chasm of love, and it hurts. But she needs to know there will be someone around who genuinely cares when her beauty fades, particularly someone who has the capacity to share human emotion, suffering and sorrow. Apollo can never offer her this.

Yet the tragedy of Marpessa's choice comes later. We know little of her life, except that she ends up alone and abandoned in her old age after Idas's death. This is a fear that most of us share. Yet even though Marpessa chose what most of us would believe to have been the right 'path', she also gave up passion, ecstasy and the possibility of what could have been a transformative experience with Apollo, by taking the 'safe' route. Marpessa never regretted living a good and compassionate life with the strong and dedicated Idas, but perhaps she may have regretted making a choice that denied her access to the realms of passion, desire, and a journey into the unknown. For the irony of her choice was that she was finally alone.

Pele and Hi'aka

Origins and Traditions

THIS tale comes from Hawaii, where the Polynesians' close connection to nature led them to worship gods who were symbolic of the forces of the earth. Thus life and death revolved around the weather and around the strange power of volcanoes, storms and the oceans.

The Polynesians seem to have originated from Asia and to have travelled across the Pacific to settle, at first, on islands like Tahiti. But their growing numbers forced some groups to move on to New Zealand and others to Hawaii. The Maoris named their land of origin Hawaiki (homeland), and most scholars agree that Hawaii is derived from this word, rather than the place of origin of these peoples being itself Hawaii.

In 1778 Captain Cook arrived in Hawaii. By 1820 the first missionaries had settled, bringing with them Christianity, which was to have a powerful effect on Polynesian mythology and subsequently on Hawaiian culture. The ruling chiefs gave up the old beliefs of their divine ancestry, the myths that they were actually related to and descended from a divine god of nature, and opted instead, perhaps with little choice, for the monotheism of Christianity. Little of their original mythology remains, and in the nineteenth century it was Western writers who chose to record and develop their own religious or cultural stories with the Hawaiian traditional ones, usually ignoring all reference to the earlier Polynesian mythology. Most of this is now lost or remains only as oral transmission in contemporary groups who have attempted to rediscover the origins and traditions of the past.

Pele, who was known as the goddess of fire as well as the goddess of volcanoes, is an important deity of the Hawaiian Islands, and she was linked strongly with the destructive image of woman. She symbolized, on an environmental level, the outpouring of lava that occurs so frequently on those islands, the changes in the weather patterns resulting from these eruptions, and the different kinds of rain that falls throughout the year. Pele became a highly regarded deity and is an excellent example of the way in which local people developed a divine projection to suit their particular geographical needs. Volcanoes must be there for a reason, and Pele, as destroyer and goddess of the volcano, must be respected and worshipped as such. This myth is, however, about the love that develops between Pele's sister, Hi'aka, and a mortal man whom Pele has already chosen to be her consort. Pele, of course, is far superior in strength, power and rage than her sister, and yet it is Hi'aka, the gentle, nurturing aspect of the dual goddess, who is rewarded by her determination to win love against all the odds.

The Myth

PELE set off from Tahiti to travel through the universe. She tucked her sister, Hi'aka, under her arm and sailed in a canoe across the ocean with the desire to journey as far as she could. When they reached the northern islands near Hawaii, lightning flashed and great bursts of energy erupted in the skies above the mountains. Here was a strange landscape: peaks that seemed too high to climb and an ocean that tumbled great crashing tides upon the shores, foam-filled and gasping as they raced up the beach. Each wave that drew back pulled with it shells and sand, and the currents were stronger than her canoe. She knew she must land or be swept back out to sea by the terror of the tides.

Pele canoed from island to island in her search for a place to live. A warm, earthy cave was all she sought, and yet each time she pushed her great body down into the earth to make an underground cavern the sea poured into the gaping hole. Every time the surging, sucking seawater filled her tunnels with sand or with shoals of dead fish as the ocean tried to drive her from every home she created, Pele became more and more violent and enraged. In frustration that none would allow her a place to stay, she stroked her sister's gentle face and wept huge tears upon her raven hair.

Eventually, Pele came to the island of Hawaii. Here the ocean could not drive her out, for some of the mountains were inland. And so it was that Pele nestled down into the great mountain of Kilauea. The mountain was solid rock, and there was no sea beneath it nor water courses or springs running through it, and that was where she lived.

But Pele was lonely. The young and beautiful Hi'aka was little company for such a powerful goddess as she. And the more lonely she became, the more she grew hungry for violence and destruction. But it was Hi'aka one night who looked up at the stars through the great chasm of the mountain that loomed above them and spoke: 'If you had a lover, Pele, then you might be happy, then you might not rage and burn with such desire.'

At first Pele would not listen to her sister's words, for how could such a young and insignificant goddess as Hi'aka know of such things? But as the nights left her feeling only anger and the days only hot desire, she began to believe that a beautiful mortal man might be the only way of preventing her from turning the island into a furnace.

One night Pele entered a trance-like state and her spirit left her body. The spirit followed the sound of music across to another island's hula dance and there took on the form of an enchanting young woman. The spirit danced with the chief's son, Lohiau, who fell in love with her. For three days they danced wildly, eagerly, the rituals and the celebrations stirring them into frenzied love for one another, until the young chief was spellbound by Pele's eager responses to his desire. Yet the time had come for her to return. The island's dance was ending, and Pele was fearful that her spirit would dissolve before him into the fire and anger of her heart.

'I must leave you, dear sweet Lohiau. For my land is untended and my fruits and my harvest will neither grow nor flourish if I do not return to them.'

'But how can I live without you? You are like a dream, a goddess! I do not even know your name... .'

'Shhh,' she whispered, placing her finger to his lips. 'Wait patiently for a few days, and then I shall send a messenger to bring you to me. Then come to me and we shall be reunited forever.' Lohiau could do nothing but agree, and, filled with the pain of torment, he watched as she slipped quietly away into the darkness.

Consumed with jealousy, Pele threw red-hot rocks across the seas

Hi'aka had spent the days while Pele had been in the trance with a friend called Hopoe, who grew lehua trees in the groves on the leeward side of Pele's mountain. When Pele returned to her body, she told Hi'aka that she must visit the young chief and bring him back. Pele promised in return that she would give Hi'aka supernatural powers and that she would, of course, look after Hopoe and the lehua trees while she was gone.

By the time Hi'aka arrived at Lohiau's island the young chief had died from love-sickness for the beautiful and mysterious woman he had met at the hula dance. But Hi'aka used the supernatural power that Pele had given her and caught his spirit as it drifted on the wind. With his spirit restored to his body, Lohiau gladly followed the girl to Hawaii.

Pele began to feel antagonistic towards her own sister and regretted having sent the pretty girl to fetch her lover. Consumed with a jealous fear that Lohiau would fall in love with her sister, Pele belched out rocks and explosions of lightning into the sky through her volcanic chasm. Red-hot streams of fire poured out all over the mountainside, engulfing Hopoe in burning rocks and molten lava and destroying the lehua blossom fields for ever.

Hi'aka's telepathic powers woke her in her sleep. 'Something terrible has happened to Hopoe. Wake up, Lohiau! We must return to my island at once!'

Lohiau, who had by now fallen in love with Hi'aka, said: 'Hi'aka, you know that I love you more than your sister! Let's return to my island and forget Pele!'

But Hi'aka knew she had to return to the island. She had promised Pele that she would take Lohiau to her, even though she had strong feelings for the chief's son. 'Whatever the consequences, we must help Pele. I think she is in trouble. As much as I care for you, I cannot betray her. You must understand that I will always love you, Lohiau, but you first loved my sister, and to her you must be true.'

Then they reached the island, and saw black smoke and burning trees before them. Hi'aka was shocked, fearful that her sister had destroyed everything. Lohiau followed her to the edge of the great chasm of the volcano where Pele lived. Hi'aka saw the destruction of her friend's blossom fields. She saw the black smoke and the burning ashes still smouldering across the valleys, and she saw her friend's corpse grey in the ashes of Pele's angry fires. Her own sister had betrayed her! She threw herself into Lohiau's arms. 'Take me away. Take me away quickly!' she cried.

But Pele, rage and jealousy spitting from her soul, had already spiralled around the two lovers with her flames of black fire and as she did so burned Lohiau to death. Yet Hi'aka's own powerful magic protected her from the violent attack, and she swirled like a mist out of Pele's burning core and rose like a plume of smoke into the sky.

For many hours she searched for Lohiau's spirit. Then, glimpsing it drifting on the wind towards his island home, she caught hold of it and returned it to his body. Together they escaped from the anger of Pele and went to live on Lohiau's island, far away from her angry fires.

Pele found better amusement for a while and forgot her treacherous sister when the hog-man came to court her. The hog-man had the power to transform himself into a pig, a plant or even a fish. While he was in human form he had created a great cloak to hide the ghastly bristles on his back and the pink ears that flopped down his cheeks. Pele teased and taunted him by calling him, 'Pig, and a son of a pig', and their conflict and disputes became more and more passionate and dangerous. Sometimes she would overwhelm him with her flames and fire, but he would throw fogs and rains over her mountains and send pigs running across her lands. Then, as the rains fell, everything would turn to mud so that her fires were extinguished.

But the gods intervened when they realized that now only the sacred fire-sticks were left alight, and they told Pele that she must compromise with the hog-man. They divided the land between them, so that Pele had places where her lava could always flow down the great gullies of the mountainsides, and the hog-man had places where it always rained, and the land was misty and damp and vegetation could grow.

Reflections

There is nothing sinister in the behaviour of Pele, for like many of us, when we feel insecure, rejected and impassioned enough about another human being, we will do anything to orchestrate the course of events. Yet Pele symbolizes the rage and destructive element in us all, and for the early myth-tellers of Polynesia, particularly of the Hawaiian Islands, the menacing side of the cyclic forces of the earth and the dark feminine mystery of woman became inextricably linked.

Pele has a sister whom she tucks under her arm and sets off to find a home. We do not know where Pele came from. It is possible that she originated from Asia, as did the Polynesian races, but she became closely associated with volcanic activity and a reasonable justification for the early Hawaiian peoples to explain the strange rumblings from the mountains and the subsequent flow of molten lava. The gentle sister Hi'aka represents the other face of Pele – kindness, compassion and human warmth. On a deeper level, Hi'aka may represent the 'higher self', that part of us that we never really get to know and that is hidden beyond the unconscious. Pele is our ego, always searching, consciously or unconsciously, for this part of the self. However, Pele is devouring, destructive and vengeful. She is driven by ferocious desires and seeks out a mate among mortals as a way of balancing her wrathful nature. The problem that gods and goddesses face when they try to relate to human beings is that mankind may worship these deities, but mankind has qualities that divine beings do not possess.

Pele changes from her probably quite ghastly goddess form to that of a beautiful woman so that she can seduce and enchant the young chief of a neighbouring island. Without much difficulty, she is able to make the mortal youth fall passionately in love, but on her departure, he tragically dies from his tormented passion. Many mythological love tales include the death of one or both of the lovers, but in Hawaii all is not lost, for the fair and gentle Hi'aka has powers of her own and is able to restore the dead Lohiau to life.

Similarly, when we go through the terrible moments of a destructive relationship or when our partner leaves us for another we may, like Lohiau's spirit, feel as if we are drifting on the wind, gusted and blown about without a sense of ever being able to touch the ground. Then it is Hi'aka, representing our own grace and integrity, who allows us to be re-born, to touch the ground and live with the knowledge that it is possible to love again.

But for Hi'aka disaster strikes. She has gone to restore Lohiau to her sister and finds instead that her own feelings are awakened. Returning now only to respect Pele's orders, she discovers that her friend, Hopoe, is dead and the beautiful mountainside is covered in black ash. Pele's jealousy has produced volcanic activity that has annihilated everything that Hi'aka loves.

This particular episode in the story symbolizes two distinct aspects of our own relationships. We often believe that nothing can destroy our love, yet devastation can, without warning, appear in many guises. It can be that we self-destruct and, figuratively, pour molten lava on our own beautiful mountainside of happiness. Our own rage and jealousy, often unprovoked, seems to rise out of our unconscious with a life of its own, devouring whatever lies in its path, like the volcanic lava flow of Pele's anger. We can lose friends, like Hopoe, and we can also lose our lovers, like Lohiau, destroyed by Pele's black and spitting flames of passion. This kind of obsessive, transformative and erotic relationship is one some of us are inexplicably drawn to, again and again. For some of us the only types of relationship we seem to have are those in which patterns of destruction, passion, anger and resentment keep recurring to keep our hearts alive. Like the phoenix, regeneration is our aim, and, like Pele, we may withdraw to the depths of the mountain to await the spark that will ignite our flames of passion once more.

Hi'aka has now once more to save her dead lover, whose spirit drifts on the wind. Poor Lohiau can survive only with the aid of the magical powers of Hi'aka, but this time Hi'aka has learned the painful truth about her sister. She has learned about her destructive behaviour and that her own trust has been betrayed. This time she leaves for another island to escape from the volcano and Pele's revenge. In a sense, she has seen the rage and violence of emotion, and has learned to chose a quieter place, an island of peace, on which love can grow.

Ironically, it is the hog-man who is able to cope with Pele and her raging volcanoes. The hog-man is just as hideous and just as destructive as she is, and his dangerous and subversive behaviour compliments and balances Pele's own. For the Hawaiian peoples, this deluge of rain and fog, the flooding of their valuable fields, could only be the result of a force as deadly and as powerful as the molten lava of Pele. Given the extremes of weather, it is hardly surprising that the gods intervened and demanded that Pele should keep to her mountainside and that the hog-man should keep to the valleys to ensure the fertility of the land. On an inner, symbolic level, we also must keep our feelings, emotions and desires aligned with our rational mind without causing chaos, without causing problems for ourselves or others. When we lose control we can destroy and self-destruct, but when we become aware and achieve equilibrium we can channel our energy across the fog-bound fields of the hog-man's plains and up the wild valleys of Pele's mountainside, hopefully with integrity.

Shiva and Parvati and the Gods of Desire

Origins and Traditions

I N EARLY Hindu mythology, Kama is the god of desire and Rati is the goddess of sexual passion. Kama's name was also known in the earlier Aryan Vedas and was identified with the creative force that grew inside Purusha when he was alone in the cosmic ocean at the beginning of time. Kama's first emanation was as desire itself, and his second as the power to create desire in others. Later on in Hindu myth he became a less powerful god and was relegated to being only the god of sexual desire, while his consort, Rati, was the female principle of the abstract and mysterious process that happens between two people when they fall in love. The following myth of the great Shiva and his love for Sati is, like most Indian tales, of epic proportion. Here, just two of Sati's many aspects are illustrated.

This story encompasses the *devas* (deities) Kama and Rati from the older cosmic order of Vedic mythology, and the manifestation of Shiva as one of the principals of the triad Ishvara, as well as Sati and Parvati, the *shaktis* (consorts) of Shiva.

The Myth

SATI had been in love with Shiva since the moment she had set eyes upon him when she was a child. She had grown up with her heart set on marrying him, even though she knew that her father, Daksha, did not approve. Daksha was the son of Brahma, and not only did he disapprove of Shiva's more destructive and wilder habits but he had come to blows with him on more than one occasion.

When Sati was old enough to marry, Daksha organized a special betrothal feast for all the gods and princes in heaven and on earth – all except Shiva, that is. Sati was convinced that Shiva would be there, and it was for her to place a garland of flowers around her chosen husband's neck.

When Sati entered the great feast she was dismayed, for Shiva was absent. In her despair, she threw the garland of flowers into the air and prayed to Shiva to catch the wreath. Her prayer was answered, and Shiva appeared before the assembly out of thin air and the wreath fell down about his neck. The furious Daksha had no alternative but to allow Sati to marry Shiva, and from then on Daksha and Shiva carried on a continuous feud.

Shiva took Sati away to the mountains, where he lived an ascetic lifestyle. He would spend many hours dreaming, meditating, and sometimes wandering around the hillsides dressed like a beggar, his body covered in dirt and ashes. Sati would follow him, wearing only rags, and Daksha was sure that Shiva led her to cremation grounds and made her dance with demons and ghosts that could not enter heaven.

Ashamed of his son-in-law's apparent dark dealings, Daksha refused to invite him to share in his offerings. Not long after the marriage, Daksha arranged for a great sacrifice and invited all the gods to be present, except Shiva. The sacrifice was to be made mostly to Vishnu, and Daksha knew this rejection of Shiva's company would hurt him deeply.

But Sati had seen the gods setting out to Daksha's palace and she ran to find Shiva, who was meditating in the wild gardens. 'Shiva, my lord! All the gods are setting out on a journey, with Indra himself. Why are you not joining them, and where are they going?'

Shiva smiled. 'Your dear father, Daksha, has arranged for a great sacrificial ceremony. He has prepared a horse to offer up to Vishnu.'

'Why aren't you going?'

'Because it has been agreed among the gods that I am outlawed from any such event. I am never to attend such ceremonies, it has been forbidden.'

Sati was furious. 'How can they do this to you? For you are part of everything, as Vishnu himself is part of everything, how can they reject you, or prevent you from attending? What can I offer or do so that you can share in this divine splendour?'

Shiva turned gently to her. 'You are very kind, but there is nothing I need from them.'

'Well, I shall go alone then, even uninvited!'

'You are Daksha's daughter, and you are always welcome in his house. But take care, for they will insult my name and curse my very being before you, and it may do more than hurt your pride.'

But Sati was angry. She did not care what they said about Shiva, for she knew him to be the one she loved.

She rode to Daksha's palace on Shiva's white bull. Her hair fell long and wild down her back, and her clothes were tattered, beggar's rags. She was received with politeness, but her father soon began to insult and deride Shiva in front of her.

'He is only a ragged beggar, a dancer of the dead! A destroyer, the ash-man! One who can only sit upon the rocks in silence. He is of the darkness and the fire.'

'But you are wrong, father!' cried Sati in anger. 'He is not what you think. He is everyone's friend. He brings life, and he is not thought ill of among the great gods.'

'There is nothing more to say to you. Go!'

But Sati could not allow her lord to be humiliated thus, and the powerful feelings she felt inside could now only sustain one thing. 'No, I will not go. I will not leave, for I am ashamed to be any child of yours! And I shall surrender this life rather own to this body that came from you.' At that moment Sati let go of the internal fire of anger and directed its energy into her heart. Spontaneously, she burst into flames as the fire rose within her and throughout her being, and she fell dead at Daksha's feet.

When Shiva heard that Sati had killed herself, he was enraged. Burning with grief and anger, he pulled out a lock of his hair and hurled it, glowing, down to earth. The hair was transformed into a terrible demon, with a body as high as the skies, a thousand arms and burning eyes as dark as storm clouds. Around his neck was a garland of skulls and, as he bowed to Shiva to ask his will, his fiery hair caused raging hurricanes across the world.

Shiva said: 'Go and destroy the sacrifices that Daksha makes, for he is no longer worthy of my time. Fear him not, for you are the anger that emanates from my darkest self!'

Sati knew Shiva to be the one she loved

90

The dreadful demon stormed through Daksha's palace, breaking vessels, insulting the priests and destroying the sacrifices. Shiva's demon decapitated Daksha, broke Yama's staff and scattered the gods, then stormed back to Shiva's side. But Shiva sat alone, in contemplation, unaware of what had happened, such was his grief for Sati.

Brahma heard of the terrible destruction wreaked by Shiva. Knowing that Shiva was capable of destroying the universe if he so desired, Brahma agreed to visit Shiva to beg him to forgive Daksha and to restore order to the gods. When they arrived, the gods found Shiva in deep meditation. He sat beneath a great fragrant tree, and as the gods implored his forgiveness he raised his eyes to them and nodded. 'Daksha is too ignorant, too naive to be a threat to me. But his head cannot be restored, so from now on he will bear a goat's head. And I shall make amends.'

Then Vishnu came, and he, Brahma and Shiva took sacrifice from Daksha and reminded him that they were the three aspects of the One. Yet Shiva could not forget Sati, and he found her body smouldering in its own self-made fire. Drunk with despair and grief, he began to dance around the earth, carrying Sati's body on his back. And as he danced, all nature withered in fear at his grief, and the soil became parched and the crops shrivelled. Vishnu knew that Shiva's dance of death would destroy the universe if he were not stopped, and so he set out to save mankind. He found Shiva dancing alone, the weight of Sati's body making his own curled and distorted as he weaved his steps through the world. Vishnu came up behind Shiva and hurled his mighty discus again and again at the limp body of Sati, until it was sliced into fifty-two pieces. With the weight of Sati's body gone, Shiva danced to the mountains to return to his eternal dream. Wherever a piece of Sati's body fell to earth, a temple of worship was built, and Shiva would shine out as the temple's guardian to all who came. But Vishnu and Brahma knew that Shiva would not rest in the mountains for long. The only thing they could do was to return Sati to life, reincarnating her as Parvati. But to do this, they needed the help of Kama.

Kama would carry a bow made of sugarcane, strung with rows of humming bees. He would fly around everywhere, shooting his five arrows of desire at both mortals and gods. These arrow heads were tipped with flowers that had been chosen by his friend Vasanta (spring), who decided which flower would be most suitable for which victim. Kama was incredibly handsome and would swoop around the skies on a parrot, accompanied by his beautiful wife, Rati, who was just as frivolous as Kama. Her other name was Mayavati, which means deceiver, but her faithfulness to Kama was unprecedented.

Kama loved to roam between mortals and gods and quite indiscriminately shoot his arrows at whoever that day took his fancy, inspiring both their desire and his own in the process. His favourite victims were usually innocent maidens, married women and celibate monks.

So Parvati was born to the great mountain goddess, Himalaya, and as Parvati grew into a beautiful young woman, she began to love and worship Shiva more and more. From her early childhood Parvati had been a devotee of his temple, often secretly making offerings and giving flowers and burning candles before the lingam. As she came of age, she was sent to be Shiva's servant, in the hope that she could awaken his desire and seduce him from his profound contemplation.

Shiva had by now turned to a totally ascetic life. Like a savage, he dressed in rags and wandered around the mountains, always deep in meditation. Observing that Shiva was interested only in contemplation and quite uninterested in the wonders of love, the gods called on Kama to arouse some passion in Shiva's heart.

Kama travelled to Mount Kailasa, where he found the great Shiva in deep silence and impervious to everything around him. He seemed almost to be a part of the great rock on which he sat. Kama hid for a while and watched as Parvati danced across the mountainside. As Parvati turned towards him, Kama pulled an arrow from his quiver and sent it hurtling towards Shiva, with the greatest, most potent flower of passion at its tip. As it struck his naked arm, lust surged through Shiva's blood, through his heart and down to his loins, just at the moment he raised his eyes to see Parvati. But even though the arrow had reached its target, Shiva also glimpsed Kama jumping for joy in his hiding place and was instantly filled with rage. As a punishment, he burned Kama to ashes with a single glance from his third eye.

Kama's spirit, however, was not dead, even though Rati mourned her lost consort. One night a voice came to her: 'Your love is not dead. When Shiva shall marry Parvati, Kama's body will be restored to his soul. Shiva's wedding-night gift to his bride shall be the union of their bodies as well as their hearts.'

But the arrow of desire worked very slowly on Shiva. For many years Shiva would not give way to his desire for Parvati, and he fought against the pull of his physical longings by intensifying his own ascetic way of life.

One day Parvati became depressed about her own beauty. What use was it to be so lovely if even Shiva did not care for her? In her anguish, she returned to the mountains and became like a hermit. She removed all her jewels and vowed to spend the rest of her life in devotion to Shiva, practising all the austerities and rituals associated with his worship. Not long after, a *brahman* youth came to her cave and admired her devotion and sacrifice to Shiva.

'Why have you denied yourself true love? You are so beautiful that you could choose anything that you desire.'

'But Kama, the god of desire, is dead. The only love I have is for the great Shiva, and so this is the only way I can assure myself that he knows of my devotion to him.'

'But he is fearsome. He is greedy, devouring and ruthless. He wears a poisonous serpent and drinks blood. He lives in the grounds of the dead and seeks to clothe the universe in darkness.'

Parvati was enraged. 'Whatever he has done will not change my feelings for him! Some things may be true of him and others false, that is all I know. But I shall love him forever!'

The *brahman* removed his cloak and revealed himself as Shiva. Together they lay in the hermit's cave. Their passion for each other was undeniable, but still it was not enough to bring love back to the world. For while Kama lay dead, Rati refused to enflame passion in the hearts of mortals or gods.

When Shiva married Parvati, the voice that had whispered to Rati in the loneliness of the night reminded her of its words. Rati immediately went to see Parvati and together they implored Shiva to allow Kama to be re-born. Shiva reluctantly agreed. He was spellbound by his love for Parvati and the sight of the beautiful Rati, and seeing that there was no fertility on earth he agreed that Kama be reincarnated as Pradyumna, the son of Krishna and Rukmani.

A great sage, Narada, advised Rati to take on the form of a mortal woman and to marry a man called Shambhara, for only in this guise would she ever be able to rejoin her beloved Kama. Shambhara, a demon in human guise, had been told by Narada that Pradyumna was destined to kill him. Shambhara was furious and stole Pradyumna, the child, and threw him into the sea, where he was quickly swallowed whole by a great fish.

For many months Rati waited for Pradyumna to appear to her, knowing that he had been born to Krishna, but he did not come. She began to give up hope and to disbelieve all that Narada had told her. One day her terrible husband Shambhara brought home a great fish he had bought at the fish market. As she gutted the dead fish, she was surprised to find inside the child Pradyumna. At this moment Narada, the sage, whispered to her: 'This is your first husband, Kama, reincarnated. I give you the power to make him invisible so that you can bring him up yourself without your husband knowing he is here. For it is your husband, the demon Shambhara, who wants to destroy him.'

'Their passion for one another was undeniable'

94

So Rati looked after the invisible Pradyumna until he was a young beautiful man, and one day told him his true identity and how she loved him. Pradyumna was horrified and could not believe her. Rati had always been like a mother to him, not a lover. But Rati made him a bow and some arrows tipped with flowers, and told him to aim one into his own foot. He did so and immediately fell in love with Rati again. For many months the couple made love in secret until eventually Rati became pregnant. Shambhara began to beat her, believing her to be unfaithful, but Pradyumna couldn't allow this to happen to his beautiful Rati, so he threw off his cloak of invisibility and killed Shambhara with his bare hands. Narada's prophecy had been fulfilled.

The couple were free, and once Pradyumna had abandoned his mortal form, Rati and Kama resumed their original forms as the god and goddess of desire and sexual passion.

Reflections

The early Vedic gods and their gradual metamorphosis into the great mythological system of Hindu philosophy constitute an epic tale that is often hard to follow. Because the Indian history of ideas has been so well documented, however, the mythology is, perhaps, more accessible than that of any other civilization apart from that of Hellenic Greece.

In Hindu myth Shiva was, simultaneously, both appeaser and destroyer. He was the lord of the dance – the dance being truth – and yet also the destroyer of life. He was the opposite force to that of Vishnu, the preserver, and whereas light radiated from Vishnu, darkness sucked all into Shiva's destructive element. Vishnu and Shiva were the two opposing aspects of the triad of Brahma, Vishnu and Shiva, Brahma being the absolute, universal balancer, the pivot. These deities were the triple-aspect of Ishvara, the ultimate One.

The confusion that often surrounds the many names of these Hindu deities lies in the fact that these apparently different incarnations and names are variations of the same aspect. The gods share the same consciousness and can appear in many different forms at one and the same time. This is because they themselves are all one aspect of the divine.

The wives, or *shaktis*, of the gods also had many names, and so Shiva's main *shakti* is Devi, and her many other aspects include Uma, Sati, Parvati and Kali. *Shakti* represents the female principle of creation and evolution, and without *shakti*, without a feminine aspect, there would be no realization or manifestation of life. *Shakti* was considered to be a more powerful principle than that of the male, representing the force of cosmic energy itself.

It is interesting to note that the three principles of the ultimate One, the polarity of Shiva and Vishnu and the balancer Brahma, form the triad called Ishvara and that the word Ishvara may share the same origin as Ishtar, the goddess of all goddesses of Babylon.

In fact, one sect of Indian worship, the Shaktas, worship Devi (or Sati) as the supreme cosmic force. To associate the absolute with the feminine is much more common in Indian philosophy than is often appreciated. The importance placed on the spiritual aspect of the Hindu woman is reflected throughout Indian mythology, and even though marriage is not based on romantic love, 'it is she with whom Shiva seeks shelter'.

The tale of Shiva's love for Sati and her subsequent reincarnation as Parvati reveals another spiritual layer. This transformation parallels the changing roles of the old *devas*, or cosmic deities, of the Vedic period, and the shifting roles of Shiva, Vishnu and Brahma in the gradual development of Indian thought.

The ancient order of gods had now to take on more spiritual and philosophical identities, and the gods were no longer seen as a means of mass control with individual responsibilities. Instead, order was maintained by polarity and balance. In a similar way, Daksha has to give way to Shiva and acknowledge that the balancing of opposites relies on there being a dark and destructive side as well as a light aspect.

It is only through the sacrifice of the female principle and the paradoxical slow destruction of the universe that order is eventually re-established. Without Sati's interference (her love for Shiva is so aroused that she causes her own soul to be consumed by flames), Shiva would not have danced his pirouette of destruction, thus causing Vishnu and Brahma to restore the balance by demanding that he be accepted by those such as Daksha. This is a highly important part of an ethical and spiritual concept: that mankind must accept and acknowledge both light and dark. Vishnu and Shiva are one, and yet it is only Shiva's *shakti,* the female principle, that creates a moment of crisis in which this can happen.

Sati's death is also reminiscent of the darkness and the destruction of fertility that occurred when Ishtar descended to the Underworld. With Sati dead and the male principle alone, there is no growth, all is sterile. His dance of death also signifies destruction from within. As Shiva whirls in a ferocious circle, he sucks in all and lets out none. The essential 'lady of the soul', Sati, is gradually broken up by the blades of Vishnu's discus, and as the weight of her memory lifts from Shiva's dark consciousness, so the world begins to lighten. Now Sati can be reincarnated as Parvati, and love and fertility will return to mankind.

The great goddess predates all gods, but she still lies dormant, an undercurrent of the cosmic force within every story, even though she has been misrepresented, misinterpreted and absorbed into the body of patriarchal myth.

Love often demands of itself a test. The story of Shiva and Parvati has many psychological implications, but the one that seems to seep gently into the light of day is how Parvati is tested, first by Daksha and then by Shiva, to prove that her love is unshakable. There may well be a more spiritual aspect to this kind of love than the romantic one that most Western hearts can comprehend. Whatever the case, the declaration of love is no substitute for action, and we see both Sati and her reincarnation as Parvati perform deeds that test their love to the limits.

Sati sees only goodness in Shiva. Whatever he represents, whatever feud causes him to fight with her father, Daksha, she is prepared to stop at nothing to defend him. Shiva the destroyer is, in a sense, a newcomer in the old cosmic order of gods and a newcomer who has, it seems, nothing to offer except destruction and darkness. As the older Vedic gods began to lose some of their power and the change to a triad of divine supremacy becomes manifest, the balance of the dark has somehow to be managed into our consciousness. But surely there is nothing 'beneficial' about such a divine concept? Both psychologically and spiritually, however, it is only when one enters the darkness that one can understand and emerge again into the light, knowing the light to be what it truly is.

Sati has no choice but to believe Shiva to be honourable and 'everyone's friend', otherwise she cannot reach the moment of transformation and re-birth in herself. Similarly, we have to trust in love and allow ourselves to be tested before we can begin to travel any road that leads us closer to knowing ourselves and finding our own 'centre'. If Sati did not have faith in her love, she would not have faith in herself. Her integrity is as much a part of her deep spiritual love as is her declaration.

So Sati kills herself, burned in her own flames of passion. Self-destruction, self-annihilation, is the only way out of the deepest darkness and the blackest night. Whether Daksha symbolizes her conscience or is in reality her father is irrelevant. Sati's love for the god of destruction is illimitable and the cost of her life is nothing in comparison.

If we view Sati and Shiva as the balancing forces of male and female within all of us, the power of Sati, the *shakti* who gives creation to all things, is here being questioned and tested, as, indeed, is the process of love. Do we honour our intuition, images, fantasies and dreams, or do we close down our right brain and listen only to left-brain logic and morality that may be alien to our own?

Sati has to be reincarnated as Parvati. Vishnu and Brahma know that without his *shakti*, without his female cosmic power, Shiva can only follow the dance of self-destruction. In our own lives, without the rhythms and cycles of nature, without our feminine soul, we often plummet into a world where we trust only the distorted reality, the veil we see before us. The goddess of illusion, Maya, enchants us and deludes us, and we deceive ourselves that we are stronger without our soul, without our *shakti* power.

When Sati is reincarnated as Parvati, her love is tested once more, but this time by Shiva himself. Meanwhile desire, the god Kama, has been temporarily destroyed and the world has become infertile and barren. Shiva has already been struck by Kama's arrow of desire, and although the potion works slowly, it still has enough power to draw the great Shiva away from his ascetic life. The darkness must sometimes erupt into the light to restore the balance in our lives. So it is that Shiva must find Parvati and test her loyalty and faith. The irony of Parvati's honour and love for Shiva, is, as she gently reminds him, that if desire is now dead, how can desire be the motivation for her compassionate love?

Here is a moment that can easily be lost within the greater context of the need to return fertility and love to the world. It is not just Kama, desire, who must return; it is Kama's union with Rati, the goddess of sexual union, that alone can bring about wholeness and the creation of new life. By himself, Kama can point his arrows and allow the abstract process of 'falling in love' to happen, but he is not responsible alone for fertility. Rati, his *shakti,* is the dual aspect, who holds the key to such power.

Parvati says: 'Desire is dead, The only love I have is for the great Shiva.' This is a different kind of love from the process of being driven by our desire. And we can see that without Kama, without desire, in the world, Parvati can still prove her love and show that some kinds of love are not motivated purely by physical desire.

So it is that Shiva must return to the light. Kama, too, must be reunited with Rati to ensure the union of their love on a physical and spiritual level. Rati has been promised that Shiva's wedding gift to Parvati will be their sexual union, thus restoring Kama's body to his soul. This dual process of the union of Shiva and Parvati and of Kama's re-birth ensures not only the continuation of love but of the creative force throughout the world.

Shiva appears to Parvati disguised as a *brahman* youth. His accusations and insults are similar to those Sati had to contend with from Daksha, but this time it is not death that she turns to but devotion and sacrifice to prove her faith. Finally, sure that Parvati's love is true, Shiva removes the cloak and allows himself to be reunited with Parvati, on one level as his *shakti* and female principle, but also as his wife and lover.

The Moon

Origins and Traditions

WHEN the first Europeans arrived in Australia they saw to it that most of the established Aboriginal culture was either ignored or rejected in favour of Christianity. The Aboriginal mythology became distorted and fragmented, and the surviving stories, which were such a major part of the oral traditions of these peoples, continued only in the ritual and song that persisted despite the European settlement.

It is claimed that humankind has been present in Australia for over 50,000 years, initially as hunter-gatherers, who lived in groups wherever the landscape enabled them to survive. The myths these people created were their direct connection to the spirit world of Dream Time. At the beginning of time, spirits travelled across Australia, creating form, plants, animals and the ancestors of every future human being. Wherever they went, these spirits left sacred pathways, stone outcrops, water holes and special places for ritual enactment, so that the inhabitants could contact Dream Time. Myths were like a picture book, or a mental road map, showing how these places could be found, and acting as a guide to how it was possible to enter Dream Time, another world and another dimension, distinct from daily existence.

The mysterious qualities associated with lunar cycles are prevalent throughout world mythology. Usually linked with female goddesses, the moon in this myth is a simple man, a human being who falls in love too easily with disastrous consequences.

The Myth

ONCE upon a time the moon was a man. Happy and with a carefree spirit, he spent most of his time dancing and whistling, singing and playing games. But there were occasions when he would fall into a black mood and become unhappy. The reason he felt so low was that he never had much luck with girls.

Although he laughed with them and loved their company, and enjoyed flirting and teasing the beautiful women of the tribe, he failed miserably when it came to wooing them. They regarded him as a fool, made jokes about him and laughed behind his back because they thought he was fat and slow-witted.

Each night he would travel across the land seeking a lover. But the tribe from which he had originated sent out a message to the rest of the land warning the other tribes that he was coming: 'Watch out, the moon is searching for a wife tonight!'

One clear and cloudless night, while the stars shone their usual messages of peace and protection from evil spirits, the moon sang a happy tune as he wandered along the riverbank, shimmering his silver light across the water. Nearby sat two sisters, who happened to hear his superb voice. They waited for him to get closer, assuming that a man with such a fine voice must be handsome and desirable. But as he approached they saw he was fat, with very short legs and thin arms. This was not the sort of man they wanted to know.

'What a weird looking man,' the girls giggled, and they ran across to the river and jumped into a canoe.

The moon saw them rowing away. 'Hey, did you hear my song? Did you hear the way I sang? Didn't you like it?'

'Yes we did, but we must go. We have to visit friends across the river.'

'Hey, won't you take me with you? I would like to come with you across the river. I'm very lonely and am looking for a girl to be my wife. Perhaps one of you two beautiful creatures might oblige?'

The girls stopped paddling, amused by this strange little man's plaintive request. 'You must be the moon. We've heard you're a flirt, and we've been told we must have nothing to do with you. So you'll have to swim across the river by yourself.'

The moon called back: 'But I'm hungry and cold. For the sake of the Pleiades and their place in the sky above, please take me. The stars would be disappointed if you cannot live up to their love for all mankind, and besides, I want to make one of you my wife.'

The sisters whispered to one another and remembered how the Pleiades shone from the sky to remind them that they must never harm any creature and love all beings. They began to row back to the shore to help the moon.

'Here, you can borrow our canoe, but you must row yourself across the river.'

'But I am unable to row, can't you do it for me?' asked the moon.

Reluctantly, the girls agreed to tow him across and plunged into the water. With one on each side, they grasped the canoe and began to struggle across the water. But the moon decided to have fun, and when they were about half-way across he began to tickle the girls under their arms. Outraged at this forward behaviour, the girls tipped the boat over and the moon plunged head-first into the deep, clear river. As he sank further and further down, they could see his shining face, big and white, becoming paler and ghostlier the further it sank. Then they could see only half his face, and eventually only a thin crescent shape was visible. Finally, his face disappeared altogether into the blackness.

The girls had recounted the story of the flirting moon to their mother, and she spread it around the whole tribe, who sent word across the country. Crow himself heard the news about the sad fate of the moon, and he called out a message to every distant land: 'The moon can no longer shine all the time. He will come from the Land of the Spirits in the west with only part of his face shining. Every night more and more of his face will show until you can see it all. Then it will gradually disappear into the east, and he will be invisible for a while. When he comes back in the west, he will peep around the corner because he is ashamed of his desire for women. But every month he'll dare to smile his watery smile and try to woo some girl in the full light of his fat face. Then he will gradually fade away because he will always be disappointed, now everyone knows about the true nature of the moon.'

Reflections

The imagery of this tale is familiar to all of us: the light of the moon is a reflected light and so is the idealized image we project on to others when we fall in love.

The moon is first a man. Then he drowns, loses his mortality and becomes a celestial manifestation and a constant, cyclic force in the lives of the Aboriginal peoples. The myths of the ancient Australian races did not consciously analyse or even record love, unlike the passionate and tragic tales from early Greek or Indian mythologies. But the simplicity of the moon's desire for a wife reflects the cultural needs of the people, as well as the individual hope and disappointment that we all at one time or another may experience.

The moon is fat and unattractive, not the kind of husband many girls would find ideal. He flirts easily and is too open about his desires. He has no grace, no heroic background and is lazy. It seems that the moon has no redeeming features at all.

Yet the appearance of the moon and its many faces had to be explained by the early myth-makers, just as did the daily appearance of the sun. In this particular tale, the sad fate of the moon-man seems an obvious reason for the waxing and waning phases of the moon. As he sinks beneath the water, his face gradually fading, distorted, hazy as he falls further and further into the deepest part of the river, we can also understand the symbolic meaning of his watery death. Like the dark days of the moon, the few days just before the new moon, this is a time when traditionally ideas are born, a time in the darkness when secrets, mystery and magic are seeded. It is a time before the first glimmer of the crescent moon when we almost have to catch our breath, to whisper instead of shout, to garner our thoughts, feelings and wishes so that they emerge with the growing, new face of the moon. The poor moon-man must undergo a similar transformative phase in his watery darkness before he can be re-born as the moon in the sky. Such is love. When we try too hard, when we push others, jump in too fast without knowing and listening to another person's values, we often lose that love and must suffer the drowning. It is this time when we must undergo the dark days of the moon before we can transform despair and loss into the purposeful growth of self.

Love both nurtures and destroys. But unlike the sad moon, if we trust in the process and cycles of life we may find ourselves able to fuse with something greater than our egotistic needs. Real unconditional love does not judge, does not blame, does not demand. Love of itself is free of words. The moon's pathway through the sky reminds us that we are bound by the cycles of nature and that we cannot escape the destiny of all mortals, but it also reminds us that while we are on this planet we can bring joy to others as well as ourselves.

The Loves of Zeus

Origins and Traditions

THE Greek pantheon is filled with rich characters and extraordinary stories, mostly because the Greek intellect was always curious, imaginative and fascinated by sharing and developing philosophical ideas. Myths travelled across Greece, and as the Greeks themselves travelled widely, they brought back ideas from such places as Egypt and Persia.

What is outstanding about Greek mythology is how it has been recorded, albeit in different versions. This happened after the patriarchal suppression of the goddess cults of the Minoan civilizations, although many of these earlier goddesses were assimilated into the Olympian pantheon. Hesiod (*fl.*800 BCE) was probably the first person to record and collect the myths concerning the beginnings of the universe and its gods, but it was Homer (ninth to eighth century BCE) who began to organize and write down the great narratives *The Iliad* and *The Odyssey*, which inspired many artists, musicians and novelists in later history. It is here, in this rich tapestry of battles and heroes, that we find deeply threaded layers of individual desire and passions, both mortal and divine, hidden beneath the personas of these sometimes quite extraordinary archetypal characters.

Apart from being the leader of the gods and ruler of the universe, Zeus had a remarkable appetite for women. Perhaps the most promiscuous of all mythological deities, he embodies the archetypes of patriarchal rule, potency, desire and power as well as the human need to play. Although he stands as a figure of pure patriarchy, there is still something inspiring about his specialness, his divine and omnipotent sovereignty of the Olympian world. But it was the power ascribed to Zeus that changed the role of women in ancient Greece, especially the re-birthing of Athene from his own head. Athene was the ancient Libyan goddess of female wisdom, and, ironically, it was originally only by devouring her mother, Metis, another aspect of female wisdom, that Zeus could lay claim to male supremacy in intellectual and judicial knowledge.

The Myth

ZEUS'S mother, Rhea, had sent the child away to live with some mountain nymphs so that his own father, the Titan Kronos, could not eat him. Kronos had already devoured Zeus's other siblings because he had been told that his children would one day overthrow him. So Rhea substituted the baby Zeus with a stone wrapped up in clothes. Kronos duly popped it down his throat, thinking he now had no cause to worry and the prophecy could never come true.

Zeus grew up in Crete with Amalthea, who nursed and suckled him. She was half-goat, half-mountain-spirit. When he was old enough, one of his sisters, Metis, the goddess of wisdom, told him how to rescue the rest of his siblings from Kronos's belly. Zeus ensured that Kronos vomited up all his other brothers and sisters, who were, of course, by now fully grown gods, and this led to the battle of the younger gods, led by Zeus, and the Titans, led by Kronos. Once Zeus and his fellow-gods had won, he exiled Kronos to Tartarus.

Zeus married twice. Because Metis had helped him initially in his struggle against Kronos, he made her his first wife. Metis was the goddess of wisdom, but when she became pregnant Zeus was told by an oracle that if the child was a boy he would be destined to become greater than Zeus himself. Zeus greatly feared this particular prophecy, because Kronos had castrated his own father, Ouranus, for the same reason and yet was now overthrown himself. As the child grew within Metis's belly, Zeus grew more and more fearful of his own fate. He therefore instigated a contest to see who could become the smallest creature. Metis, who always liked a challenge, immediately turned herself into a fly. Zeus grabbed her out of the air and swallowed her, and her immortal wisdom merged into the body of Zeus as he digested her fly-form.

But the trick backfired on Zeus to some extent, for later that evening he developed a terrible headache. The sounds thumping inside his own head were so violent that he called Prometheus and Hephaestus to help him. Prometheus held his head while his blacksmith son, Hephaestus, performed an emergency operation and split open his head with a wedge and hammer. Suddenly out sprang Athene, the goddess of wisdom and war. But because she had not been born in the normal way and because she was not male, Zeus had nothing to fear from her. In fact, it was Athene who provided the strongest support to Zeus and never betrayed him.

His second wife, Hera, was a different matter. Like Metis, Hera was also Zeus's sister, but she had been unhappy about not having any share in the initial division of power in the universe and had stormed off to Mount Thornax, where she lived in the wilderness and sulked alone. For many months she saw no one, and then as spring came and the mists rose she found a bedraggled cuckoo. She took pity on it and put it to her breast to warm it up. At that moment the cuckoo turned into Zeus, who instantly made love to her. He persuaded Hera to come to his kingdom as co-ruler and to be his consort, but she was always jealous of Zeus's wandering eyes and also acutely aware of the trick he had played on her at Mount Thornax.

The only time Hera ever had more power over Zeus than he had over her was when she borrowed Aphrodite's girdle of desire. This made any mortal or god instantly infatuated with the wearer. Zeus enjoyed Hera all the time she wore the girdle, but Hera could never forgive Zeus for his promiscuity, and she began to detest him. Eventually, she persuaded Poseidon and Apollo to conspire to overthrow him.

So that Zeus did not have time to get hold of his mighty thunderbolts, the two gods crept up while he slept and tied him to his bed with ropes of cattle hide. These were unbreakable, and not even the mighty Zeus could escape. But this trap caused chaos on earth, and Thetis, the ocean nymph, visited the Underworld and released the Hundred-handed Giant who rushed up to Olympus and set Zeus free.

Zeus's revenge on Hera was predictable enough. He used golden chains to tie her upside down to the sky and weighted her with anvils so that her limbs stretched and her body ached. He left her for over a year and finally cut her down, forcing her to grovel at his feet.

Among Zeus's lovers was the forest nymph Callisto

Now that his throne was secure and he was sure of being the supreme ruler, he left the running of the universe to all the other gods and

spent most of his time in pursuit of beautiful mortals. Every time he spotted someone who took his fancy, he would take on some appropriate disguise so that he could have sex. In fact, Zeus mated with Titans, birds, animals and even clouds and running water, and it was said that his offspring from mortal women were the ancestors of the human race. Hera was constantly bitter and resentful, and would often pursue Zeus's lovers, either seeking vengeance on their offspring or on the women themselves.

Among Zeus's lovers was the forest-nymph, Callisto, who was Artemis's companion. She loved Zeus and bore him a son, Arcas. But she was changed into a bear, either by Hera in a fit of jealous rage or by Zeus himself to save her from the evil deeds of Hera. Unfortunately for Callisto, while she was in bear form, she was shot by her own friend Artemis who was hunting in the forest and was placed in the constellations as the Great Bear by Zeus as a sign of his love for her.

Europa was another of Zeus's lovers. She was the daughter of Telephassa and the king of Agenor in Phoenicia. One spring day she went out in the fields to pick flowers with her maids near the king's cattle. Zeus disguised himself as one of the bulls and let the girls play with his horns and fondle him. Europa was precocious and daring, and she decided to ride the bull. But the bull plunged into the sea with Europa on his back and disappeared across the ocean to Crete. The bull took her on to the sand, raped her and left her. Europa bore three sons, Minos, Rhadamanthys and Sarpedon, and then married the local King Asterius. Asterius was not too pleased at marrying a woman who was not a virgin, and so Zeus agreed, as a compensation for Europa's 'imperfection', to give him a great bronze man called Talos to defend his kingdoms.

Danae's encounter with Zeus was more of a life-saving mission. She had been imprisoned in a bronze tower by her father, Acrisius, king of Argos, because he had been told by an oracle that Danae would be the cause of his death as he would be killed by his grandson. To prevent Danae from ever having a child, Acrisius locked her away in the bronze tower, with no food and only one slave to bring her water.

Zeus's lusty eyes could see everything. He spotted Danae in her tower and immediately decided she was in need of his attention. He came to her as a golden shower of rain that poured through the roof of the tower. After a night of rampant sex, Danae conceived and bore a son, Perseus, but the slave heard the baby crying and told Acrisius. Fearful that his life was in danger, the king ordered that Danae and the child be put into a wooden box and thrown into the sea. But the box was under the protection of the gods, for no mortal can destroy Zeus's child unless Zeus so wills it. Perseus and Danae were safely guided across the sea by

Poseidon to the island of Seriphos. A fisherman, Dictys, caught the box in his net and took Danae and Perseus to live with the king of the island, Polydectes. After many adventures, Perseus did, in fact, kill his own grandfather by accident when throwing a discus in a competition.

Zeus was tempted by the sight of Semele, the daughter of Cadmus and Harmonia. For many weeks Zeus visited her in the guise of a mortal, and Semele, who was besotted with Zeus, began to boast to her sisters about her affair with the great god. Zeus seemed to be totally in love with Semele himself, and she soon conceived his child. With the intensity of passion firmly aroused and established, Zeus promised her anything she wanted, and to confirm that this was a genuine pledge, he made a vow in the name of the River Styx. Gods were forced to obey this promise and never to break their word. This was such a powerful gesture of intention, that Semele knew he would never go back on his oath.

But Hera found out about Zeus's liaison and decided to intervene. Taking on the form of an old servant, Beroe, Hera suggested that Semele wasn't getting the full benefit of Zeus's love-making skills. After all, he was the supreme god and in his divine form he must surely be the greatest lover, better than any mortal. Why not suggest that Zeus came to her in his full immortal radiance and splendour, not disguised as just an ordinary mortal creature? Wouldn't that be the ultimate glory? Semele was suitably excited about meeting the god in person and also wanted to boast to her sisters that she had slept with Zeus in his divine form. So Semele sent a message to Zeus, asking him to come to her in his full radiance. Zeus did not want to do this and would have refused, but he had made a promise and had to fulfil his pledge to her.

When he appeared to her in his full immortal glory, he was like the very sky itself. Thunder and lightning radiated down, and fire shot through Semele's body and entered her like a thunderbolt as they made love. This was just as Hera wanted – Semele was incinerated by the fire of Zeus's own passion. In Semele's dying moments Zeus managed to snatch the tiny embryo and save it from the raging inferno of his own fire. He placed the baby in his thigh until it reached full term. This child was Dionysus. Once he was elevated to god status, Dionysus visited the Underworld to recover Semele and immortalized her as the goddess Thyone.

Leda was married to the king of Sparta. She was one of the most beautiful mortals that Zeus had ever seen, and when he spotted her bathing in the River Eurotas he was instantly filled with lust. But Leda was already carrying the Spartan king's child and was known to be incredibly faithful. There was only one way to ravish her, and that was to trick her into making love with him.

Zeus asked Aphrodite to help him. He transformed himself into a swan, and Aphrodite changed herself into an eagle. Together they soared across the sky like the hunted and the hunter until they came to the clouds above the River Eurotas. Zeus swooped down and fell on to the water as if he had been chased by the eagle, and the eagle swooped down and then soared back up into the air as if it had been cheated of its prey. Leda took pity on the swan and took it into her lap, where she stroked and comforted it. As soon as Zeus felt she was languidly mesmerized by petting the swan, he had sex with her, took off into the air and disappeared. After a while Leda gave birth to two swan eggs. Out of one were hatched Clytemnestra and Helen; out of the other came Castor and Pollux. It was not known exactly who was the father of which child, but Clytemnestra and Helen became mortals and stayed on earth, while Castor and Pollux were treated as immortals and taken up to heaven. When Leda died, she was taken to heaven and was merged with Nemesis, the goddess of retribution.

Io, a river-nymph and daughter of the river-god Inachus, was a virgin priestess to Hera at the temple in Argos. When Zeus first set eyes on this beautiful nymph he arranged for Io to be taken from Argos so that he could seduce her away from the watchful eyes of Hera. He changed Io into an exquisite cow, but Hera guessed immediately what he was up to and asked Zeus to give her the cow as a present. He could hardly refuse without revealing the truth, and Hera's first punishment for Io was to keep her tethered among all the other cows in the muddy fields. She sent the Hundred-eyed Argus to keep guard over the cow and stop Zeus from rescuing Io. But Zeus was not to be stopped from having the river-nymph, and he persuaded Hermes to go down to the fields and sing and play a lullaby to Argus, who eventually fell asleep. Hermes then stole Io from the herd and gave her to Zeus.

Hera was mad with rage and jealousy when she heard what had happened, and she sent a gadfly to sting the cow so that it would never stand still again. Io went mad from the constant pain of the stinging fly and ran around the world trying to escape from the terrible agony. She wandered even as far as Mount Caucasus, where she saw poor Prometheus chained to a rock for stealing fire from the gods.

Her punishment lasted for many months, but at last her torment ended when she came to Egypt and Zeus made love to her on a cloud. She returned to her normal form and the fly disappeared. Surprisingly, Hera finally forgave her. Io bore a son to Zeus, Ephasus, who was a calf-child.

Zeus and Io

Reflections

Whatever the historical ramifications or the spiritual implications of the end of the great goddess cults and the establishment of the new male deities, Zeus, the great patriarch of Greek mythology, represents, thanks largely to the writings of Hesiod and Homer, one of the richest symbols of elitist passion.

Whatever his vices or virtues, Zeus was as terrified of 'fate' as any mortal. His own upbringing was as fraught as any human's, and the oracles that revealed he might be overthrown, just as he overthrew his own father, Kronos, made him resolute in his conviction that his supremacy would never be taken from him. It is worth considering that Metis, his first consort and sister, whom he swallowed because of this very oracle, was in earlier, pre-Hellenic mythology known as Medusa. Both goddesses symbolized female wisdom. Perhaps the patriarchal, Zeus-led pantheon could assimilate this aspect of the goddess only if Zeus absorbed the wisdom principle himself.

Zeus's own myth is reflective of the changing culture at the time. Around 2200 BCE the worshippers of sky-gods took over in the Greek islands. Before this was the Greek Bronze Age and a culture known as the Minoan period. The Minoan culture worshipped the earth goddesses, but by about 1200 BCE the final overthrow of the Minoan culture was complete and the last known place of fertility and earth-goddess cults were dissipated in Crete. So the lunar, earth-based, matriarchal culture transformed to a solar, masculine-dominated consciousness. It was a shift that was part of a natural evolution of collective changes from one culture to another.

In a sense, Zeus and his rise to power provided a new mythology. The archetypal quality of this god can give rise in ourselves to something that wants to create a new order within. In this respect Zeus had some awareness of mortal suffering even though he seemed blind to the suffering he himself caused.

This great archetype often surges into our own daily life without our knowing we are carrying him. For Zeus can manifest as the great know-it-all, or the colleague at work who has always got luck on his side, or the elitist. At an extreme, Zeus can work his way out into the world by becoming a religious fanatic or someone who believes they are a god. In the world of relationships he appears mostly in the guise of the passionate romantic rather than as the warm, earthy sensualist or displaying the ordinariness of mortal love.

Zeus is born into a difficult world, filled with oracles and determined by fate. He must rise above this to be special, and he does. That is why so often in relationships we may assume that we are more important, more divine than the person on whom we have projected this uniqueness. Zeus must, above all, prove himself to be above justice. In fact, Zeus could do anything he wanted.

When we are devoured by the Zeus archetype, he fills our relationships with such tremendous power that we often believe that we, too, can do anything we want, that we are above morality, laws and the personal morality of others. We are omnipotent and special, our egos are inflated, and we believe we have luck on our side.

Zeus is a womanizer, but he draws the universe further and further into an amoral maze. It is only Hera who seems able to trap Zeus by persuading Poseidon and Apollo to tie him down in his bed. Hera, quite rightly from her own point of view, is consistently jealous of Zeus's dalliances. Finally, she takes extreme measures, as we often do when those we love seem to challenge our inner and outer security. But because Zeus is the supreme god, his entrapment means that the earth falls into chaos, and he is only released by Thetis, the cool, serenely compassionate ocean-nymph and mother of Achilles. Zeus had once longed to make Thetis his consort, but he had been warned off by another fateful oracle.

The image of tying Zeus to a bed, symbolically an attempt to repress solar consciousness, is as negating as repressing the lunar, feminine consciousness, just as the Hellenic patriarchy stamped out the goddesses of the Minoan era. It is the harmony of male and female, and the balance of both within each of us, that may ensure we do not need the help of the Hundred-handed Giant from the Underworld.

Thetis is like a voice from our soul, telling us that we must remember there are times when we have no choice but to reach down into the darker realms to unleash those feelings which can return us to our place of power. The Hundred-handed Giant comes to our aid when our lunar, receptive side, our 'Thetis', hears our arrogant solar side cry for help. Zeus was fortunate that there was a woman around whom he had not yet betrayed who would still help him. Many of his later lovers might have turned their backs on his plight.

Hera's anger becomes Zeus's revenge. Zeus takes it out on Hera by weighting her with anvils and tying her upside down to the sky, thereby ensuring, symbolically, that feelings are punished rather than being acknowledged. Zeus has literally hung her feelings up on the sky of solar rational dogmatism. There are many women, just as there are men, who enjoy this same exercise of power over their partners or lovers, by hanging them upside down, or rather by 'putting them down', in front of friends, family and even strangers. By undermining a partner's own self-worth with our own inflated sense of importance, we exclude the possibility that anyone else might have their own perception, their own values. Zeus can be ruthless, as can we all when our divine child becomes scared of losing its personal power.

But once Zeus begins to feel comfortable, once the divine child within us feels wanted, safe, perhaps settled in a simple human partnership with another, strangely and unexpectedly it is often time to go out and play again. For Zeus this was easy. He was one of the most promiscuous of all gods in any mythology, and it is hardly surprising that Hera became portrayed as a spoil-sport and sour-puss, just as any woman who identifies with this pattern in a relationship is so portrayed.

Yet Zeus was divine and special. He was above morality, even his own, and he was also a traveller, an explorer, a god on a quest. His personal quest was to find himself through the many women, mortal and divine, with whom he fell in love. Falling in love is a spiritual and significant moment, and Zeus was able to use his extraordinary charisma and his ability to shape-shift to any form to seduce, ravish and often rape whomsoever he pleased to achieve this kind of grandiose self-pleasing. However, this is Zeus gone wrong; this is Zeus in love with himself. But this *is* Zeus, and it is his dark side.

Throughout the stories of his numerous love affairs we find Hera in the background, ready to make trouble. But what is it that she represents? She is not just an angry wife, betrayed and frustrated by the promiscuity of her divine consort. Does she represent our conscience? Is it the voice within that tells us that by falling in and out of love, by demanding physical satisfaction and giving nothing in return, except moments of divine madness, we are not really loving, but just testing our power? Hera represents not only law and morality, but our ability for meaningful relationships, for trust, mutual sharing and loyalty.

The foolish and gullible Semele is a character with whom many of us can identify. She begins a passionate liaison with Zeus in his guise as a mortal. She knows who he is and knows he is married to Hera, but like many of us, Semele wants more from him. She wants him for herself. Her expectations are high, just as our own may be when we first believe we have truly fallen in love with 'the one who can fulfil all our needs'. If they are already married or attached to someone else, they may seem more desirable, more idealistic.

Goaded on by Hera, who has disguised herself as the servant Beroe, Semele demands that Zeus come to her in his divine form. Zeus has already promised her anything she wants and has no choice but to comply, knowing full well what the outcome will be. True to form, he arrives as a bolt of lightning, which strikes right through her, and Semele is incinerated in the flames of his divine passion.

This is where the solar principle goes wrong. For if we gratify ourselves by giving way to sexual desire alone, we may find that the intensity of passion does not last. Semele wanted too much. She got the full force of Zeus's divinity, but it killed her. The relationship was doomed to end, as many of our own torrid physical tangles seem to do. It is interesting to note that Dionysus, the instantaneous embryo of this fiery union, was saved and carried in Zeus's thigh until he reached full term, for it is Dionysus who carries the archetype of ecstasy, the transcendence of earthly pleasure – the very experience that Semele wished to sample with Zeus.

Dionysus, like Athene, is born from Zeus's body. Athene, who came from Zeus's head, is the bringer of female wisdom to the Olympian pantheon, a wisdom she inherited not from Zeus but from her mother, Metis. Both Athene and Dionysus predate the Olympian gods and had established cults during the Minoan Bronze Age. Yet they had to be 're-born' in the solar patriarchal consciousness – in other words, they had to be born through Zeus alone so that they could be ingested in a more rational form than their previous lunar, seemingly dark cult images. The older, earthier goddess worship was totally inconsistent with the laws of the sky-gods.

The desire of Zeus is the purist form of the desire of the gods. This archetypal force that surges into our own lives, often as if from nowhere, is uncontrollable, fantastic and compelling. Without it we would not experience moments of ecstasy or divine energy surging through us. The paradox is that without desire we become filled with exactly what desire breeds in us, namely egotism and self-gratification. As noted in the Introduction, the word 'desire' comes from the Latin *de sidera*, 'the absence of stars'. When we have no stars to guide us, no points of reference, no compass, no human measurement of morality, humanity and structure itself, we are left to be driven by the gods. For the gods do not live by the stars, they have no laws, boundaries or maps to plot their lives. They have no feelings. So desire takes us over like the gods, and the desire of Zeus is the most potent, the most physical and the most driven. By developing an awareness of desire and of the energies that seem to flow uncontrollably within us, we can perhaps experience the insatiable desire of Zeus, but through a reflective, lunar awareness rather than a solar mind that has become rigid and blinkered by the very civilizing principle embedded in our western psyche over the past four thousand years.

The Herdsman and the Weaver-girl

Origins and Traditions

CHINESE mythology evolved and modified continually throughout the history of this vast and ancient culture. It was connected to the great systems of thought that began with the early Taoist philosophy from the sixth century BCE and the later introduction of Buddhism and Confucianism, which latched on to this ancient belief system, thus adding and enriching the Chinese tapestry of myth with an ever-increasing array of gods, beasts and weird and wonderful creatures. Like many other ancient mythologies, the celestial realms and creation had first to be explained, and the gods or goddesses who became the planets or the stars in the sky were revered and worshipped formally and informally with the rise of the dynastic kingdoms of the great emperors.

This is the tale of Altair and Vega, the two fixed stars of the Milky Way, and how they came to be there.

The Myth

THERE lived in the sky a weaver-girl, whose beautiful robes were adorned with sparkling stars. The girl wove all the clouds into different coloured threads, and it was her job to make the rainbow clothes and hang them in the sky. She had to weave many different garments for every kind of weather. It might be pink and peach for warm, sunny days in spring, or red and crimson for sunset autumn, or black-violet and grey for winter storms and rainy days. This part of heaven was called the Silver River, and it was a shallow stream that ran across the sky, just touching the earth in one place where reeds and rocks created a heavenly pool. Across heaven, at the far end of the Silver River on earth, lived a young herdsman who had been orphaned when he was a child. He worked all day long in the fields with his ox as his only companion.

As the boy grew into a grown man, one day the ox spoke. He told Ni Lang about a weaver-girl and her friends who bathed each day in the Silver River. They came from heaven and were the most exquisite creatures ever to be seen. If the herdsman could steal the girl's clothes while she was bathing in the river pool, she would be his wife. So the herdsman travelled down to the bank of the Silver River as darkness fell, and he hid among the reeds and tall bulrushes that grew close to the still, shallow water. Not long after dusk the weaver-girl and her friends arrived to bathe. They threw their clothes on to the rocks and jumped happily into the clear water. The still water of the stream sparkled as it ran off their backs on to the rocks, and the herdsman was hypnotized by the beauty of the weaver-girl. Entranced, he watched them for a while, then, realizing that they would soon be coming back to the rocks for their clothes, he quickly dashed out from the reed-bed and snatched the weaver-girl's clothes. The other girls heard the noise in the bulrushes and were terrified. They began to run away naked but the weaver-girl stayed all alone, wondering who it could be hiding in the reed-bed.

'Come out,' she called softly. 'It's all right. I won't harm you.'

The herdsman crept out from the long reeds and with his face down – he dared not look at her nakedness – he said: 'Here are your clothes. I'm sorry but my ox told me to steal your clothes, for then you would become my wife.'

The weaver-girl laughed. 'Yes, you will have to be my husband now you have seen me without my clothes.' Ni Lang looked up and instantly fell in love with the weaver-girl and they were married.

For a long long time they lived happily together. Ni Lang worked in the fields, and the weaver-girl wove her clouds. They had two children and a happy home, and it seemed that nothing could come between them. But the perfect union they had found on earth could not be.

The god of the heavens and his consort found out that the weaver-girl had chosen to live on earth, and they demanded she return immediately to the palace of heaven to be punished. Before Ni Lang had returned home from the fields, she had been taken away from her family. The herdsman was devastated when he found her gone, and placing their two children in panniers on a pole across his back, he set off towards the Silver River, to the place he had first found her, hoping that she might be there.

But when he reached the rocks there was no river and no pool. The angry queen of the heavens had stolen the river and taken it up to the sky together with the weaver-girl. As the sun set below the horizon, Ni Lang looked up and saw the bright band of the Silver River now far away in the sky, so that mortals and gods could never meet again.

All night he tossed and turned in his despair. But with the morning came the ox to his side. 'I am dying, herdsman. Once I have departed this form, wrap yourself in my skin and you will find that you can get to heaven.'

So the ox died that day and Ni Lang wrapped himself in the heavy skin. Then a transformation occurred! He felt that he had wings and that he was lighter than air. He put the children in his panniers, pushed a ladle through the two baskets so that he could carry them behind him and flew up into the sky.

Beyond him were beautiful stars, shimmering gleams of twinkling colours that filled the Silver River with light. In the sky, on the other side of the Silver River, the children saw the weaver-girl and called to her: 'Mother, mother, we have come to you!' But the herdsman was unable to cross the river. The great goddess of the heavens had taken one of her long hairpins and gouged a great gash down the middle of the river so that it changed from a shallow, gentle stream to a raging torrent. It was so deep and so dangerous that there was no way the herdsman could cross it now.

Ni Lang wept with despair and anger, but his daughter said: 'Take the ladle, father, and drain the river until there's no more water in it.'

So the herdsman and his children took turns with the ladle, scooping the torrents of water out of the riverbed. The god of heaven had watched them trying to reach the weaver-girl, and he felt sorry for the poor herdsman and compromised. 'You may visit the weaver-girl once a year, but that is all I can do for you.'

So the weaver-girl and the herdsman lived on different sides of the river. The weaver-girl is Vega and the herdsman is Altair. Every seventh

*The Herdsman and
the Weaver-girl*

118

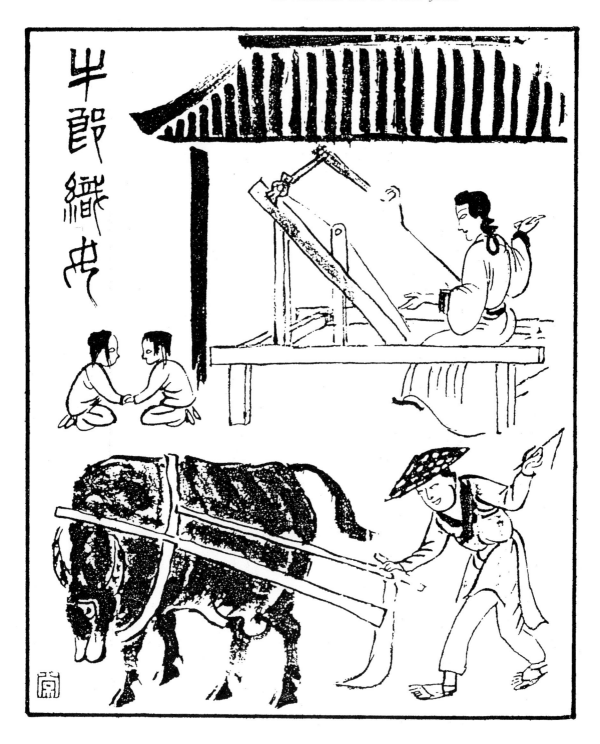

day of the seventh month the herdsman crosses a bridge that is made by flocks of magpies that soar across the Silver River. Then the herdsman and his children cross the bridge, and he makes love to her again. When they embrace the weaver-girl cries and her tears fall to earth. The women on earth know she is crying because her tears fall like soft drizzle from the clouds she has painted grey.

So Vega and Altair are on different sides of the river, and the four bright stars beside him are the shuttles of the weaver-girl's loom, and the two stars on each side of him are his children. Beside the weaver-girl are three bright stars, which are the messages from Ni Lang. And when you see these bright stars in the autumn sky it is to remind us of the eternal love between the weaver-girl and the herdsman.

Reflections

The Milky Way fascinated ancient peoples the world over, but none so much as the Chinese. Many different Chinese myths refer to the Milky Way as the source of the great Yellow River. If a man first travelled along the Yellow River then journeyed along the Milky Way (the Silver River), he might eventually reach the great Celestial River that flows around the universe. The Milky Way was the bridge between the mortal world of physical reality and the spiritual world of eternity. For those in the eastern hemisphere this giant bridge of light in the sky was as powerful an image as the sun and moon.

This particular mythological explanation of the two stars Vega and Altair has female and male principles, Vega being female, the weaver-girl, yin, and Altair being male, the herdsman, yang. In Taoist philosophical belief yin and yang must be balanced before spiritual enlightenment or physical transcendence can take place. Taking a journey along the Milky Way relied on the subtle involvement of the two stars in polarity.

The herdsman acquires wisdom and knowledge through the ox, a symbol of sagacity in the East. He tells the herdsman that if he were to capture the heart of the weaver-girl he would attain great happiness. The herdsman falls in love and all seems likely to proceed as the wise old ox had foretold. But by choosing to marry an immortal girl the herdsman has, as with most divine/mortal unions, caused overwhelming chaos. The heavenly gods are displeased and demand that the weaver-girl return to the sky alone. The herdsman now has no choice but to listen again to the wise counsel of the ox, which must die before the herdsman can continue his journey to the Silver River. In symbolic terms, the ox's death and the herdsman's journey along the Milky

Way are reminiscent of an inner rebirthing, when we must face some new crisis, some change in our perceptions of the world before we can continue renewed and self-aware. It is not that our egos must be shed completely, but we must discover a new awareness, an enriched perception, before we can go forward.

The ox, or the old ways of the ego, must be transformed for the new. The herdsman can make his journey only if he wears the magical skins to help him. He must suffer if he is to complete his mission to find the weaver-girl, and he must learn that love requires effort as well as projection.

Yet on reaching the Silver River there is no way that he can cross it. This is the finality of human love: it cannot become divine; it cannot become any-thing other than what it is. And the realization that he can go no further allows him to love in the only way he can, from a human heart.

The gods concede a monthly visit, and these two fixed stars either side of the Milky Way are given physical purpose and spiritual and mystical balance.

Bitiou's Revenge

Origins and Traditions

THIS short but blood-thirsty myth of love and vengeance dates from the thirteenth century BCE and the reign of one of the greatest pharaohs, Ramses the Great. Some sources suggest it dates back even further, to 4000 years or more.

This extraordinary civilization believed that life was a gift from the gods, and its dynastic empire ruled for nearly three thousand years. Egyptian life was rooted firmly in its mythology, and the evolving civilization actually incorporated their main mythic beliefs into the religious structure, which in turn formed a whole belief system based on the original mythology of the gods. Pharaohs and their families were believed to be incarnations of known deities, or even new and variant gods. The grander the dynasty, the more widespread were its related myth and religion.

In all Egyptian mythology the initial creator encompassed both male and female gender and qualities but ironically was only seen as a male deity. However, the serpent-goddess symbolism became a powerful antidote for the weighted male creator-gods of the patriarchal dynastic periods. Both Isis and Nephthys were serpent-goddesses and represented both the world above as well as the Underworld. Thus Egyptian consorts of the pharaoh often wore cobra crowns. Their status was paradoxically far more important than the goddesses upon which they modelled themselves.

The succession of pharaohs depended exclusively on the marriage of the pharaoh to his sister or half-sister. This was because the gods only married their goddess sisters, and if the pharaoh was an incarnation of a god, he could only follow this particular rise to power and royal right. Mothers, too, were far more important than their sons. For each pharaoh had to have been conceived by the seed of the sun-god, and thus the mother must have had sex with the sun-god for the son to claim his right to be pharaoh. However, the mother could never become pharaoh herself.

The following tale vividly reflects the cultural importance of this right of succession. It also reveals how the shadowy depths of human experience can be sparked off from simple betrayal, and how revenge sometimes is sweeter than we dare to believe.

The Myth

JUST before the great golden sun set below the horizon, a youth named Bitiou led his cattle into the barn for the night. The leading cow suddenly stopped at the door and began to make a lowing noise. Bitiou knew the language of animals. He had learned to understand every lowing of the cow, each grumble of the goat and each song of the birds from the moment he was born. He held the rope tightly, pulling back the cow as he listened to her words: 'Watch out! Your brother Anapou is waiting behind the door! He has a knife!' Bitiou saw the shadow of Anapou flash past the door just as the last rays of the sinking sun swept a golden sheath of light across the stone ground.

He let go of the cow, turned quickly and began to run for his life. Not understanding why his brother had been waiting to kill him, he sensed the fear of death in his heart urging him to escape. When Anapou saw the cow unattended, and Bitiou's footprints in the dust, he ran quickly after him, knowing that he was stronger and faster than his younger brother. But the sun-god, Ra, took pity on Bitiou. Ra saw everything and knew everything that happened in the world. Creating a huge, deep river that gushed its way across the desert between the two brothers, Ra decided to save Bitiou from his death.

Bitiou caught his breath and stopped, sensing that Anapou could no longer catch him. He stood defiantly on the other side of the raging river, waiting to hear abuse from his brother. Anapou cursed the river and shouted across to Bitiou: 'You deserve to die, I should have killed you and I still will if I ever catch up with you again. My wife says you raped her!'

Bitiou couldn't believe what he had heard. He had never touched Anapou's wife nor even given her one glance of lustful desire. There was no reason why Anapou should have said such things about him. In his anger and horror, he cut off his own testicles and threw them into the river for the fish.

'Your wife is a liar! I'm going to travel far away so that I never see either of you again. I am ashamed to know you as my brother and for you to believe these things she has said about me. But if you ever find the wine in your cup becomes cloudy, then you must come to help me.'

Anapou was overcome with guilt about his misjudgement. How could his wife have accused his own brother of such a thing? Distraught and filled with grief that Bitiou had vanished, he ran home in a frenzy. The knife he had sharpened to kill his brother gleamed in the sunlight. Ra had obviously saved his brother for some purpose, and now his knife had to find a new home. Anapou crept back into his house and before his wife could turn round to face him, he pushed the knife deep into her neck.

Bitiou travelled for many days. He had become more and more distressed about the behaviour of his brother, and the accusations of his sister-in-law. His feelings were wounded, and he vowed that he would never allow anyone access to his heart again. So he took his feelings and his heart and hid them in the trunk of an acacia tree, knowing that no one would ever find them there.

The potter-god, Khnum, felt sorry for Bitiou in his loneliness and decided that he needed a consort. As a potter it was easy for him to make an artificial girl out of clay. He placed her near the river and because she smelt so beautiful, when she washed her hair the river became perfumed with the most wonderful fragrance, like the blossom of the acacia tree. Bitiou was instantly enchanted by the beauty and the overwhelming scent of the clay girl and she became his bride. Because he trusted her he showed her where he had put his heart and his feelings for safe-keeping – inside the acacia tree.

For many months the girl would wash her black hair in the river, and for many months the perfume drifted downstream towards the palace of the pharaoh.

The pharaoh became fascinated by the lingering perfume and decided to find out who it was that was casting such a powerful spell over him. As each day passed he yearned more and more to find the creature who was making him hungry with passion. The pharaoh and his court took the barge and rowed upstream for many days, further and further into the wilderness. Many wanted to turn back, but the pharaoh's only desire was to find the girl who had enchanted him. When he finally found the clay girl, he decided there and then that he would marry her. The artificial girl could only see herself now as the pharaoh's queen.

Bitiou had travelled further up the river to catch the pearl fish that they ate for breakfast. The artificial girl knew she would have to act quickly before he returned: 'Pharaoh, I would gladly be your bride, but I cannot unless you cut down that acacia tree. For I am bound by its power.'

The pharaoh took an axe from the barge and began to hack at the great tree-trunk. Sweat ran down his back, down his forehead and into his eyes. With each swing of his body the tree began to creak and tremble, until it finally toppled over and hit the ground. At the moment the acacia tree was felled, Bitiou died too, his heart and his feelings totally destroyed inside. Many miles away, Anapou was drinking his favourite wine. As the red liquid turned cloudy, Anapou knew his brother was in danger or, worse, was already dead. Anapou stood up quickly and walked away from his drinking friends, vowing to find his brother. It was time to make amends for all the unhappiness and sorrow he had caused Bitiou.

For seven years he travelled across Egypt, through the baking hot desert, across the barren countryside and the wilderness, searching for his brother, and then one day he came to a riverbank where an old tree had been felled. Along the water's edge were some dried-up acacia berries from the tree. Anapou sensed this was where his brother's heart lay, and he picked up the one berry that still smelt fragrant and placed it in a cup of water.

A white light began to glow from the water, until the berry, the cup and the light turned into a great white bull, pure and radiant. This bull was Bitiou.

Bitiou had no choice but to go to the palace of the pharaoh and confront the artificial girl. He didn't want her back, but he had trusted her with his secret and she had betrayed him.

The artificial girl had become the pharaoh's queen. When she saw the white bull arriving at the palace gates she recognized him immediately as Bitiou and was terrified that he had come to seek revenge. She ran to the great pharaoh, knowing that he would do as she asked because he loved her so much.

'Will you do anything for me, anything in the world, and if I ask something of you, will you promise to do it?' she said breathlessly.

125

'You know I will do whatever your heart desires,' he said, mesmerized by her charm.

'There is a great white bull that has come to the palace. You must kill it, for it has come as a sacrifice to Ra.' The pharaoh nodded; he did not want to kill the unusual beast, but he had no choice but to honour his promise to the girl.

So the pharaoh took his knife and slit the bull's throat. The blood gushed across the ground and flowing from it were two seeds of the persea tree. Within a few years these trees grew so tall that people began to worship them as if they were divine gods. The shade of these two trees became a sacred place for all the pharaoh's subjects to make sacrifices and honour their gods. But the artificial queen was not happy, for she knew that in the trees lay the soul of Bitiou. This time she did not ask the pharaoh to help her. She sent for two foresters and ordered them to cut down the trees. As she stood watching, the light of her inimitable power dancing in her eyes, a tiny chip of wood flew from the woodsman's axe and landed between the queen's smiling lips. At that instance she conceived a son. The child that was born was none other than Bitiou.

So the artificial queen gave birth to the husband she had murdered in his first incarnation as a man, had murdered again when he was a bull and again as a tree. The years passed and she did not know that her son was Bitiou, and when the pharaoh died Bitiou became the pharaoh, for he had married his sister and was the son of Ra.

Bitiou knew he could not trust his mother, the artificial girl, and so he sent for his brother, the only one in whom he could believe, the only one whose love was unquestionable. He made Anapou prince of the Nile and brought his mother to trial before all the people and told them how she had tried so many times to destroy him, because all she had wanted was wealth and riches and had never loved anyone. She was a woman ravaged by greed, and the price she would now have to pay was her execution.

Reflections

The story of Bitiou seems to raise many questions that concern not only our relationships with others, but our relationship with ourselves. There are two major symbolic levels here: first, the cultural/spiritual theme, concerning the right of succession and the inextricably linked belief in reincarnation, and second, the individual psychological one, the right to be loved for who you are.

If we look at Bitiou's apparently humble beginnings we already know he is destined to be someone of great importance. He can understand the language of animals, and as he flees from his brother's anger, the great god Ra suddenly saves him. In Egyptian civilization magical powers meant you were in touch with the gods or, at best, were possibly an incarnation of a god. The intervention of Ra also meant you might be descended from the great god. Perhaps Bitiou is an aspect of the great sun-god himself. Whatever the case, here Ra's omnipotence is unquestionable, and the power of the gods will always overcome the insignificant tangles of human relationships.

Bitiou castrates himself when he is accused of lying with his brother's wife. Whether he does so out of shame or out of bitterness, the possibility of his divine inheritance means that his own mortal seed is neither necessary nor convenient for the strange means by which he achieves pharaohdom. There is also an interesting parallel here to the story of Osiris and the loss of his genitals in the Nile. Although Isis recovered the missing phallus and impregnated herself with the seed to give birth to Horus, eventually the worship of Osiris's phallus became hugely popular. Egyptian women would carry images of Osiris's penis about their person. Osiris represented the virile male principle, and was usually represented with his sexual member exposed in exaggerated erection.

In this story Bitiou loses his male potency, but as the story continues it is through reincarnation that his power is restored and his redemption complete – as with Osiris. Osiris was also originally worshipped in his aspect as an ox, and only later assumed human form. We see Bitiou reincarnated into a bull, the most potent and virile image of all Egyptian procreative and phallic power.

However, it is Horus, the son of Osiris, who receives the favour of Ra and also ruled Egypt as the first pharaoh. This is perhaps the closest alignment to Bitiou's own fate. Each pharaoh in succession was a reincarnation of Horus. When a pharaoh died he automatically left to merge with Osiris in the Underworld, while the pharaoh's son would also become a new Horus.

Here Bitiou has somehow to become pharaoh by his own process of reincarnation in three forms, man, animal and vegetation. Again, another symbol of the ancient fertilization myth of birth, death and re-birth of the natural world.

Bitiou here encapsulates all the elements of the Egyptian philosophy of reincarnation: as Osiris, when he loses his genitals in the fertilizing waters of the Nile; as the white bull, who must be sacrificed; as Isis, the very 'heart' of the acacia tree; and as Horus, the pharaoh's son seeded from the tree that the pharaoh himself had felled, to become Horus, the eternal eye of Ra.

The artificial girl is not unlike the role that the mother or sister must play in the succession line, the paradox being that it is only through her wicked deeds that Bitiou can become pharaoh. The artificial girl is both mother and consort. First, she is made by the creator-god Khnum, but cannot produce any heirs because Bitiou has castrated himself. Therefore she has no choice but to marry the ageing pharaoh to produce heirs. Ironically, her treachery is the only means by which Bitiou can reincarnate and leave behind his seed. The acacia tree holds his female principle, or Isis, his soul. When Bitiou's acacia tree is felled, he dies. Without the female aspect he is unable to live. With neither his male potency, nor his soul, he must die to be born again. Aided by his mortified brother (possibly Anapou is a parallel to the protagonist brother Set in the Osiris–Isis–Horus re-birth myth), he is transformed into a highly potent bull. Now terrified, the artificial girl plays the role of devil's advocate again until finally Bitiou reincarnates as her own son. A direct connection to the belief of each pharaoh as a reincarnated Horus, waiting to become Osiris.

Although this myth displays the deep-held ancient Egyptian belief in reincarnation and the powerful connection to the cultural mythology of the time, it also illuminates several facets of the human psyche at work in the polarity of love and hate.

We do not know why Bitiou's brother accuses Bitiou of seducing his wife, and it may be that Anapou and his wife are purely a symbol of the side of ourselves that carries envy, greed or anger. But Anapou's appearance right at the beginning of this myth plummets us straight into the shadowy world of Bitiou's unconscious. However, he must save his own life from the knife held by the hand of a real-life brother with vengeance on his mind. This is like being thrown into the middle of a soap opera when you have seen none of the earlier episodes. For Bitiou and Anapou must have had their own story to tell, and yet they have no time to explain. There is only time for Ra, the solar principle, to come between their dispute. As with our logical, left-brain thinking, it is usually this kind of conscious awareness on which we chose to rely in moments of crisis. Anapou is left to take vengeance on his wife, the true source of his anger, and Bitiou, strangely, to cut off his own maleness. Whether Bitiou cannot come to terms with his true guilt or whether his disbelief is so great that his brother should wrongly accuse him is not clear. But the symbolic castration seems to point the finger at his own desires, and it is this particular dismemberment that forces him to search more thoroughly for answers. Self-castration also symbolizes self-doubt and one method of finding the feminine side of the self. Even Ra castrated himself so that a new race came forth from his blood.

Bitiou's story is essentially one of losing trust, first, in the blood bond of his brother, and second, in himself. Feeling hurt and betrayed, Bitiou hides his heart inside an acacia tree. We often do this in our own way. We hide our feelings from others, grow a hard exterior and protect our vulnerable side from harm. We surround our heart with our own sweet-smelling acacia tree, but often the sap inside becomes stale and sticky. For Bitiou, the arrival of the artificial girl gives him a chance to see his own sweet nature in her. A prime projection – and a moment when he falls in love. The artificial girl is made by a god, she comes from nowhere, and like the mysterious thing it is, love surges into Bitiou's life with extraordinary consequences. The revelation of where his heart has been hidden is the cause of Bitiou's fall from grace. Attempting to trust another person, Bitiou allows his feelings to be known, and immediately he is betrayed. After all, if Bitiou is castrated, falling in love with an ideal is one thing, but to keep up the strain of such an impossible love means that the relationship has to change. The change comes with the arrival of the pharaoh. The artificial girl becomes attracted to someone who seems to have more to offer, physically, than Bitiou. Bitiou has 'travelled further up the river to catch the pearl fish', and in a sense has himself gradually moved away from the girl both literally and psychologically, as happens in many relationships built merely on an initial physical attraction.

Then the girl betrays him; the tree is felled, because she knows it is his heart that keeps her there. She believes she is being emotionally blackmailed, and without the tree Bitiou can no longer keep her. Without the tree of feeling, Bitiou can no longer live. His male solar principle, literally his genitalia, he himself sacrificed, and now his female principle, his soul, has been destroyed by the intervention of the pharaoh.

The symbology of this story is complex, and more space might be needed to analyse the intricacies of this myth, yet the transformations that Bitiou must make – his three reincarnations – suggest the pain and suffering he must undergo in order to become whole. Within the context of Egyptian religious and dynastic society, Bitiou becomes a pharaoh through the process of reincarnation. In a psychological sense, he becomes pharaoh because he has earned himself worth and value. He has suffered, he has been re-born three times and he has learned about love. In this way his is able to take on the role of pharaoh. Bitiou sends for his brother at the end of the story, and his mother, the artificial girl, has now to face her own judgement. Unknowingly, she has given birth to him and thus Bitiou is released from the romance. The death of his mother, the artificial girl, means perhaps he has let go of the projection. He has found his own anima, his own soul within. The artificial girl was an illusion, an illusion that he created and now can leave behind. He can begin to understand who he really is and, through the betrayal of love, he learns to love himself.

Eros and Psyche

Origins and Traditions

THE story of Eros and Psyche has inspired writers, artists, poets, musicians and even psychologists. This haunting tale of a woman's love for a god carries the essence of both the divine and the human ways in which we love. It also reminds us how the ancient patriarchal Greek culture viewed women and how these views and opinions are still alive within our modern Western society.

Many fairy-tales owe their plots to Apuleius's version of the story, which was part of his work *The Golden Ass*. But the myth of Psyche and Eros had an oral tradition in ancient Greece long before Apuleius recorded it in the second century BCE.

Eros and Psyche's allegorical symbolism is rich, and at its deepest level it is a superb analogy of the journey of our own souls through the pain and terrible tests of being human. The transformation we must all undergo to become who we really are and to discover our inner world is magically brought to life in this myth. *Psyche* is the Greek word for 'soul', and many writers have used this allegory as a framework for investigating the female personality. Jung used the words *anima* to describe the female soul in men and *animus* to describe the male spirit in women, respectively, but 'soul' and 'spirit' are part of the balance of male and female in each of us, whatever our gender. Every woman has within her *anima*, just as

130

every man has *animus*. It is the way we relate to these energies that matters and the quality of these energies that manifest themselves in our outer world. Like the Taoist belief in yin and yang, both are energies that form the whole. It is Psyche and Eros, as male and female, who best represent in their relationship the gradual awareness and awakening of the wholeness and unity within each of us.

The Myth

THERE once was a kingdom, and in the place lived a beautiful girl, the youngest of the three daughters of the king of Miletus. Such was her beauty and such was her grace that the people began to adore her more and more as she grew up into a young and serene woman. Her name was Psyche, which means 'soul'.

But because many men idolized her beauty and others dared not even think they might be worthy of her love, she lived a lonely and isolated life. Her two older sisters married well and found good husbands in royal households, yet Psyche was treated like a goddess, until even the ordinary people began to believe she was more important, more divine and more beautiful than even the great Aphrodite herself. But for Psyche this caused only much unhappiness, for no man attempted to be her suitor for fear of her wondrous powers.

'See, she is a mortal, and yet her looks are more ravishing than Aphrodite. Here is a new goddess who lives among us, to take the place of even Aphrodite,' proclaimed the people.

When Aphrodite heard these rumours and saw that men were forsaking her temples and worshipping this mortal woman, she became greatly angered. With vengeance in her heart, she sent for her son, Eros.

'This is an outrage! How can it be that a mortal woman is being worshipped in my place? You must go down to Earth and pierce Psyche with one of your arrows so that she might fall in love with the first beast or ugly old man that she sees! Make sure you shoot your arrow at the very moment she is to come across such a ghastly being, to ensure she never receives grace nor honour from men again!'

Psyche's own father was much concerned that she had not yet found a suitor and so on that very same day that Aphrodite spoke to Eros, he visited the oracle to find out what fate lay in store for his daughter. But the oracle had been duly commanded by Aphrodite to reveal that Psyche would marry an evil spirit, a beast who roamed the mountain tops. Psyche was to be taken to the top of the mountain, clothed in her bridal gown, and chained to a rock, to await the ravishment of the dreadful creature who was like death himself.

When Eros arrived on earth he found the beautiful Psyche on the way to the mountain top to await her fate. There were many mourners, a long procession trailing across the darkening landscape as evening came. As Eros took another, closer look at Psyche, he accidentally pricked his finger on his own arrow, such was his amazement at her beauty, and he instantly fell in love with her.

Alone on the mountain, Psyche was fearful as her father and friends sorrowfully abandoned her. Yet it was not long after that a breeze began to swirl around her, gently at first, and whispering, 'You must come to me, you must come to me,' as it blew cool air across her brow. For Eros had asked his friend the West Wind to carry Psyche away from that terrible place to his own palace. So enamoured, so wretchedly in love with this mortal was Eros that he wanted her to be his bride. Yet Eros had betrayed his mother's command and now he had no choice but to hide Psyche away, for Aphrodite would surely destroy her if she discovered their love.

The wind carried Psyche for some time, she knew not where, then gently she was set down, in paradise it seemed. Here was a magnificent palace set in a valley carpeted with wild flowers and great trees. She was given a feast by invisible servants, bathed in crystal water and shown robes and a golden chamber where she might sleep. Psyche was still fearful, unsure who it was that guided her, uncertain if the stranger who owned this sumptuous place was indeed an evil spirit. That night she lay awake, watching the stars. In the darkness Eros came to her; she felt his hands upon her skin, gentle hands, not those of a beast or of death. With soft caresses he calmed her spirit, and they melted into love together. Their blissful union was unlike no other, and now Psyche could only marvel at the tenderness and passion of this invisible husband.

As she rose to light the lamp, he touched her hand and whispered: 'No, dear Psyche, you must never look upon me and must never know who I am, for if you see me, this magical place will disappear and I can never return.'

'But you are my husband, can I not see you, cannot I now share your love in the daylight?'

Eros sighed. 'No, this can never be, for great danger would befall us both if you did this. I will return each night, for our love is unbreakable.'

'He saw the burn on his shoulder and flew away in terror'

So for many nights Psyche was content with this, for she had everything a woman could want: the magnificent love of a god, it seemed, and the beauty and luxuries that she could never have in a mortal marriage. Yet as time passed, the days became lonely for Psyche, and she longed to see her family again. She asked Eros if they might visit her and reluctantly he agreed, for his love for her was such that he could not deny her such a simple request. He still feared the wrath of his mother, however, so he agreed to Psyche's request on condition that she never tried to find out his identity nor revealed how deep was their love, for if she did so he would leave her for ever. 'If you should find out my true identity, Psyche, the child you are to bear will be a mortal and a girl. If you do not question, do not listen to other people's wild accusations – for there will be many – you will bear an immortal son.'

So the sisters came to the same crag from which Psyche had been wafted into paradise by the West Wind, and they too were lifted by the gentle winds and carried to the golden palace. They were pleased to see Psyche and marvelled at the magical gardens, the fine clothes and the beautiful surroundings. But after two or three visits they began to grow envious and jealous of Psyche's riches and god-like lover, whom they never saw. The sisters began to grow curious about the identity of this seemingly perfect husband. After each visit, when Eros came to her alone at night, Psyche would puzzle over their thoughts and he in turn would warn her not to trust them, for fear of her discovering who he was.

On the fourth visit they demanded to know more about him. 'Who is this wondrous husband of whom you speak? And where is he, Psyche? How can you trust this man, are you not worried that he may be a monster, some terrible serpent come to ravish you? This lover-husband of yours must be hiding some foul secret, or he would show himself to you. Come, Psyche, do not be fooled. Make sure you reveal his face tonight. Light the lamp and gaze upon him while he sleeps, so that if it be that he is some monster, you have a chance to escape.'

'You are only jealous, because he gives me so much and because he loves me so!' she cried, as they prepared to leave.

'There is only one way to find out if we tell the truth or if he does. You must take a knife with you to the bedchamber, and once your husband sleeps, light the lamp and, if he is truly evil as we fear, sever the head of the fearsome monster with whom you have bedded. There is no other way to find out the truth, is there, Psyche?'

Psyche was troubled by conflicting feelings all day. She did not want to betray her promise to Eros, but she feared that her sisters spoke the truth and she must unmask him, to find out if he were truly a monster or

a demon. That night, therefore, she lit the lamp and held a knife tightly
to her side to kill the monster if indeed he were so. She approached the
bed and as the light glowed across it she saw the sleeping god of love
himself. In astonishment, she gazed down on the beautiful creature, and
her guilt for betraying him overwhelmed her. Here was the god of love,
Eros himself – he was her lover and her husband! She fumbled with the
knife and as she stooped to pick it up, pricked herself on one of Eros's
arrows. She had fallen in love with him. Turning to go without a sound,
her hands trembling, her heart pounding with her foolish fantasies and
the betrayal of her promise, a drop of oil fell from the lamp on to his
naked skin. Eros woke suddenly from the pain. He saw the burn on his
shoulder and flew away in terror. Now that Psyche had seen him and broken her promise, he was fearful of Aphrodite's revenge if she should ever
find out.

With Eros gone from her, Psyche suffered from feelings of terrifying
remorse at what she had done. She had broken her promise, she had
believed the silly lies of her sisters, and now she had lost everything,
including the god who had loved her enough to defy even his great
mother. Inconsolable, she set out to find her lover, and she travelled
wearily across the lands towards one of Aphrodite's temples. There she
begged the goddess to help her. At first, Aphrodite admonished her,
refusing even to look upon the mortal who had upstaged her. But when
she found that Eros was deeply unhappy, wretched on his bed and pining
for his lover, she relented and offered Psyche the chance of regaining his
love by completing four tasks.

'Psyche, there is one journey you can take to find immortality and be
united with your lover, but it is a journey of tests. Are you prepared to
travel on this path?'

Psyche was still filled with despair, but hastily and bravely agreed.
What choice had she now but either to kill herself or to take courage and
try to restore her love with the god? It was a chance she had to take.

'Your first task is to sort out the great pile of mixed seeds you see
before you into their individual piles. You must do this before night
comes, or the penalty is death.'

So Psyche began to sort the seeds, but after some hours she realized
the impossibility of the task and lay down, weeping pitifully, for she was
convinced that she must die as she fell asleep. But as she slept, an army of
ants, sent by Eros, passed by. The ants took pity on Psyche and began to
sort the seeds, a task they had completed before nightfall. Aphrodite
returned and grudgingly had to concede that Psyche had done well.

'Your second task is to gather some fleece from the golden rams of

135

the sun. They graze across the river, in the fields over there. You must accomplish this before dawn.'

Psyche knew that this was a dangerous and almost impossible task, for the rams were fierce, aggressive and violent. Gentle Psyche could not bear to think about her fate, and as she drew near to the river, she collapsed in despair beside the reeds. But one reed spoke, whispering to her as she lay in her fearful state: 'Go to the edge of the field when darkness falls, for all along the brambles and hedgerows their fleece is caught in bundles; you can take it from there while they sleep.'

So Psyche did as she was told, and she took the bundle of golden fleece to Aphrodite, who looked darkly upon her. 'So, you have skills in magic that even I cannot know! If you are artful in such magic, this task may be worthy of your skill,' she smiled. 'Next you must fill a crystal goblet with water from the River Styx. This is the water that has no source and yet no sea to fill, for it comes from high in the mountains and falls between great rocks into the bowels of the earth to the Underworld. There is no place on land from which you can reach it, for it is guarded by high cliffs, rocks and dangerous beasts.'

The waters were wild and unreachable, and Psyche tried to clamber across the great rocks but slipped many times down the cliffs, thinking she must die. Yet an eagle of Zeus appeared as she fell with her goblet, struggling to keep her hold on the rocky ledges. The eagle flew down to her and, taking the goblet from her hands, dived down into the chasm of turbulent water and filled it for her.

When Aphrodite saw Psyche return to her clutching the goblet filled with the magic water, she became angry. Dark was her demeanour, and terrible deeds filled her heart. 'This is your last task, Psyche. You must go to the Underworld. Take this casket and find Persephone, the queen of the Underworld, and ask her to fill this casket with beauty. But you must neither help anyone nor under any circumstances must you open the casket. You must deliver it only to me, for beauty has more power than you can ever imagine!'

To Psyche, this task seemed now the most difficult. She stumbled across the fields and, coming to a high tower, climbed up it so that she could throw herself from it, such was her despair. But as she stood on the tower, ready to throw herself to her death, the tower itself spoke to her: 'The path you must follow lies yonder. There you will find the entrance to the Underworld. But you must take two pieces of barley cake in your hands, two coins in your teeth and courage in your heart; only then may you return with the casket of beauty. But do not open it, on any account, for that may be the biggest lie.'

Psyche's despair

So Psyche set off to the Underworld. The barley cakes, the coins and her courage made sure that she could reach the deepest part of the Underworld and return. Persephone herself took the casket then returned it to Psyche, the mystical secret now contained within. Again, she fed Cerberus the dog with barley cake and paid the ferryman with her coin. But as she reached the entrance to the light and stepped into the upper world, the temptation to open the casket was too great for her.

'Why should Aphrodite lay claim to this beauty? Why should I not take some for myself? It was my beauty that Eros loved and so that Eros might find me beautiful when we meet again, shall I not take some of this mystery for myself?' So Psyche opened the box to find out the mystery of the beauty within. But there was nothing inside except sleep. This strange vapour rose like a mist before her face and overcame Psyche, who fell into a deep and deadly sleep.

But Eros had recovered from his burn and had learned how his mother had put Psyche to the test. Knowing that only he could save her, he flew swiftly to where she lay. As he gazed upon her lovely face, he realized that Psyche was the only one he loved. He lifted her up, gently pricked her with one of his love arrows to wake her and, tenderly wiping the sleep from her face, placed it back inside the casket.

When she saw her lover Eros before her she could only offer her lips up to him. And then silver and gold wings sprang from the shoulders of fair Psyche so that she could fly towards Olympus with the god of love. There Aphrodite looked upon her with smiles, not anger, and Zeus offered her the goblet of immortality from which to drink so that she might live with Eros forever. And so it was that Eros and Psyche were united in marriage before the gods, and not long after a daughter, Pleasure, was born to them.

Reflections

There have been many attempts to analyse and reveal the deeper levels of this ancient story of a woman's love for a divine being. At its simplest interpretation, we can see how Psyche wants what many mortal women and men want: to fall in love and live happily ever after. However, first, she must learn about herself. She must learn to find love within herself and love for herself before she can truly have a life-long relationship or, in Psyche's case, an eternal relationship with a god.

The beauty that makes her enchanting and a powerful attraction in the world of men is only a surface beauty. Psyche must seek and find the true beauty within, for then she may love another being, whether divine or mortal, as well as she loves herself.

Psyche, who is beauty personified, threatens the power of Aphrodite. But this beauty is something human, not divine, and Psyche is unaware of the power she has, for it seems that she leads a lonely life with no hope of finding a partner. Many of us today choose beauty, looks and fashion as a way of stating who we are. But this surface grace is only another mask that we wear and that we all share. The Greeks, the Romans, the earlier Bronze Age civilizations, indeed, as far back as we have records of mankind, beautified the body. Our bodies are our shrines, for they are the form through with which we can honour any deeper sense of Self. Beauty has been an essential part of fertility, attraction, ritual and spiritual transcendence throughout the world. Adornment is part of our lives, but it is still only skin deep. We often assume that what we project on the surface, or rather what we see others to be, is a true representation of what lies within.

For Psyche, the journey to find beauty is the journey to find out what love is all about. So what is our inner beauty? It is a mystery, it is hidden, untouchable and unknown. It is our souls and it is our passion, it is our desire, it is our deepest unknown territory. Beauty is a quality that gives pleasure to the eyes, but our sense of it, paradoxically, emanates only from this place of beauty within. The poet Robert Bridges wrote:

> Live thou thy life beneath the making sun
> Till Beauty, Truth and Love in thee are one.

This is Psyche's journey, and every human being has the potential to take this journey, too.

Aphrodite's disapproval of Psyche's new-found power leads her to turn to Eros to perform a terrible deed and to make sure that the mortal girl falls in love with a dark monster. Through an oracle it is decreed that Psyche is to meet her fate upon the mountain, and she has no choice but to meet what is probably 'death himself'. In a sense, the moment we fall in love is like 'death himself': we are overcome by a powerful force that seems alien to our rational minds, and we feel caught up in some drama that is nothing to do with our own lives. Falling in love is the greatest mystery we can ever experience, which is often what makes it so addictive. We feel that time no longer exists, and we feel that we have 'been here before' and that we have met this person in some other life, in some other time. 'Love' seems to comes to us without warning, without conscious choice. Psyche has no choice when Eros visits her, for Eros himself, the god of love, falls in love with her beauty because he pricks himself on his own arrow of desire.

139

Much has been written about Eros and his origins. In earlier Greek mythology – Hesiod's *Theogony*, for example – Eros was born out of Chaos and was a primal god at the beginning of time. He helped to bring the world into creation and only later reappeared in the Olympic pantheon as the son of Aphrodite and Ares. He was the god of erotic desire, representing the powerful emotional and physical trigger that sparks passion, while his arrows symbolize the moment of falling in love itself. Although Aphrodite also represents love and sexual pleasure, she is more concerned with the reality, with the relationship and the creative aspect of love, of putting the erotic principle into practice. Eros is the divine force that overwhelms us. Aphrodite must do something with it.

So Psyche and Eros together represent that growth within each of us, the union between divine and human love. Psyche unknowingly begins her own journey. Through consciously relating, by becoming aware of her inner needs and the awareness of the feelings of another being, divine or not, she can reach the deeper levels of human relationship.

We are all born with a beautiful capacity for life. But Psyche's is to her detriment rather than a blessing. From the beginning, Psyche's physical beauty means she cannot easily relate to another human being, for those who see such beauty must, by the very nature of human envy, judge accordingly. On another level, all the time she is married to the invisible partner, Eros, Psyche does not get in tune with her deeper emotional needs nor with her ability to communicate. The beauty of her soul has yet to shine. And it is not until she falls in love 'accidentally' from Eros's arrow, that she realizes the awful error she has made.

We, too, are often guilty of being blind to our partner's love. He/she is often invisible to us, hidden from our eyes by the magical devices of an illusionist. But the illusionist is not the partner, it is our own self.

Eros must hide Psyche from the watchful eyes of his mother. He sends the West Wind to carry her to his palace and, knowing he must not reveal himself to her, appears night after night as her lover, insisting that she never gaze upon him. This is the Eros principle at work, and we may find it familiar. When we first fall in love we don't want to 'know' the person, we don't want them to 'know' us, for then the magic, the timeless quality of this state may be broken, and unconsciously we don't want to lose touch with this powerful force that is, in fact, coming from within. The human equivalent of Eros being unmasked would be our illusions turning to disillusion. The stark and often flawed face we now see before us no longer holds the magic of our souls, and our partner becomes just another human being.

But Psyche has not yet 'fallen in love' with Eros. She has doubts about who this 'god' really is. Her sisters, perhaps representing her conscience, her fears and her inner anxieties, come to haunt her. They demand that she gaze upon the face of her lover, expose him for the evil monster he probably is and then kill him. Not only does she not trust his love for her, but she does not trust herself. She comes to Eros burdened with family complexes, with the terrifying oracle of a dark demon as her spouse. No one has ever assured her of the light and no joy has been hers, until these nights in the dark with perhaps only imagined love.

When we are insecure, fearful of rejection and fearful of allowing 'Eros' into our lives, we may hold back, driven by our doubts and fears, and demanding more from that person than they are capable of giving. We want sacrifices, we want proof. We want Eros to unmask himself so that we can be sure. But Psyche's mistrust is both her downfall and the first step on her journey towards finding her own soul, her own 'beauty, love and truth as one'.

She lights the lamp, dishonouring Eros's trust while listening only to her fears. When she finds before her the god of love himself, she has no choice but to fall in love with him. It is often when we realize we have doubted someone else, when our own assumptions or our own pride cause another to give up on us, that we invite Eros to come in through our window. Psyche falls in love with Eros when she pricks herself on his arrow by mistake, and her 'foolish fantasies' are now revealed for what they are.

But Eros now rejects her. She has betrayed him and broken her promise. Of course, like many lovers, Eros is hurt and cannot bear the pain he must now face. The dreadful truth dawns on him that Psyche has human faults. The burning oil and the light before his eyes are reality. Psyche is, after all, only mortal – she makes mistakes, she can err, she is not divine. When we are in love we expect our lover never to be a real human who makes a mistake or misjudges us, or to reveal themselves to be an imperfect being. When a partner transgresses our own idealization of how we think they should be, they, metaphorically, spill burning oil on our skin to burn us. It seems as if they were doing it to destroy our Eros principle and the relationship!

In order for Psyche now to restore her own relationship with Eros – and with herself – she has to undergo a series of tasks. Aphrodite represents for Psyche her own ability to relate, to hold a mirror before her and learn to give pleasure and to take pleasure: to connect to another person. All these things Eros alone cannot help her with. She must go to Aphrodite and suffer for her love and for her own soul. Eros is the agent of love, but Aphrodite is the active performer.

Many writers have suggested different symbolism behind the tasks that Aphrodite sets Psyche. The sorting of seeds being the sifting of thoughts, of the rationalization process, she must first go through. The stealing of the golden fleece may be seen as representative of taking only what is freely available without removing another's right to their own power. The rams are aggressive, and so the dynamic force that activates Psyche has to learn to use another force, that of receptive feminine acceptance. In this way, we can be inspired to find an alternative to active confrontation.

Filling a goblet with the water of life is a metaphor for inviting feelings to enter our hearts. Yet we are warned not to take too much on at once, no more than we can safely carry. Zeus's eagle has greater vision and a keener eye than any human being. We may have to take on our journey the eagle's foresight to help us know how much we can take and the best vantage point from which to fill our cup. The eagle represents the acquisition of a wisdom that enables us to acknowledge feeling for what it is.

The journey to the Underworld is the last and most crucial task. This is a journey few of us would actually take because it relies not only on discovering our spiritual nature and our darker side, but also the awareness that we all have our own lonely exploration to undertake. Psyche cannot tarry in the Underworld. She must acknowledge Persephone, who symbolizes her unconscious female darkness, and return quickly before she becomes trapped in a spiritual dead-end. She is given the box of beauty without question by Persephone – perhaps the goddess of the Underworld knows the real truth behind its contents – and to return the mysterious casket filled with Persephone's beauty is a powerful symbol of bringing back the beauty from within.

But Psyche is not convinced that Aphrodite can lay total claim to the beauty, for she wants some herself – just enough to attract Eros back into her lonely and painful life. But Psyche has still not learned. She still believes that changing her make-up with a box of beauty is the only way to win Eros's love. Similarly when we discover our inner ability to relate, we may deny ourselves the chance to show that we can do so. By not offering up the box of beauty to Aphrodite, in a sense we are not yet giving of ourselves truly to another, we are not yet truly relating. To keep the casket only for oneself is not to bring about the merger of beauty, truth and love; it is to estrange them even further.

Psyche came into the world already armed with enough physical beauty. She was adored by men but lonely because no one would dare to come too close. Thus far her beauty had been lived only externally, but through the love of Eros and the inner journey towards self-awareness, Psyche might begin to glimpse the real beauty within. So Psyche takes the box from Persephone in the Underworld, she brings it out of the darkness of her unconscious. But she cannot give it to Aphrodite, she cannot let it be. Because it is all so fascinating and mysterious to open the closed lid, she momentarily loses touch with grace. Opening the closed lid of the box paradoxically closes the lids of her open eyes! For now a dangerous sleep overwhelms her, the price she must pay for not trusting in the process that Aphrodite has awakened in her. Sleep means she is now truly unconscious, blind to real human love in a world of dreams.

Eros must come to Psyche's aid. For it is only love that can save her from this path upon which she seems fated to travel. To become filled with sleep is to be filled with non-awareness. To live only in a spiritual landscape is to lose touch with our self. So Eros comes for her, wipes sleep from her face and pierces her with one of his arrows. This is the moment when she experiences love, both erotic and divine. Eros has literally awakened her own 'erotic' nature, enabling her to find a connection between divine and earthly love. Plato once wrote that love is passion aroused by beauty. And here Eros, passion, is also aroused by the true beauty of Psyche, the soul.

Psyche is made immortal, and from the union of Eros and Psyche the child Pleasure is born. *Chambers Twentieth Century Dictionary* defines beauty as 'the quality that gives pleasure to our eyes'. Is it possible that the eventual union of Eros and Psyche creates the beauty that we truly seek by bringing the child, Pleasure, into our lives? For giving pleasure to our eyes is also giving pleasure to our souls, for our eyes are the windows to our soul. And is not our soul, Psyche, at the same time, the very place from which beauty shines?

Scar-face

Origins and Traditions

THE Algonquian people of North America were widespread in the forests and plains of the north, from the source of the Mississippi at Lake Itasca in Minnesota, the heartland of this linguistic group, across to Ontario, through Dakota and Montana and to the furthest western edge of their territories beside the Columbia River and the Rocky Mountains. Like many other tribal peoples, these different linguistic communities originated from groups spreading from Asia on to the American continent over 10,000 years ago. The Algonquian peoples included tribes such as the Fox, the Delaware and the best known of all, the Blackfeet.

This tale draws on both the deep association with the natural world, especially the sun and the moon, in these people's daily lives and on their own pride and cultural heritage.

The Myth

SCAR-FACE was one of the bravest of the younger hunters in the tribe, but many braves teased and taunted him because of the ugly scar across his face, which had ruined his good looks. Indian girls refused to look at him, such was his terrible disfigurement. The scar had been the result of an encounter with a grizzly bear, but although Scar-face had courageously killed the beast, he had been left only with this sad reminder that he was a mighty hunter.

Scar-face had fallen in love with the chief's daughter. All the young hunters in the tribe wanted to marry this beautiful girl, and many had declared their love to her. But Scar-face was miserable. Why should such a wonderful creature like the chief's daughter want such a poor and disfigured man like himself?

One day Scar-face walked past her as she sat weaving outside her lodge. He stopped and looked deeply into her eyes, hoping that she might return his gaze. She gave him one quick look from behind her long eyelashes and then ran down towards the river, terrified of her own feelings for him, yet knowing him to be ugly and scorned.

One of her past admirers had been suitably rejected, and he saw the exchange of glances between the couple. He followed Scar-face down to the edge of the encampment, then strode up to him with a sneer on his face. 'Hah, Scar-face, so you want to marry the chief's daughter, do you? Now's your chance, but do you really believe you've got more of one than I?'

'I may have a blemish on my face, but not in my heart,' replied Scar-face and left to find the girl. He ran quickly down to the river, where he knew she would be pulling rushes to make baskets. Scar-face sat down beside her and spoke quietly: 'I may be poor, but my heart is filled with love for you. I've got no furs, no riches, but I live by my bow and spear. Would you marry me and live with me in my lodge?'

The girl looked at him directly now, and he felt as if the sun was shining out of her eyes. But she hesitated. 'My father has much wealth, so it is not necessary for my husband to be rich. But the sun-god has decreed that I shall never marry anyone, for I am to be his own sun-maiden.'

Scar-face was sad. 'How can this be? Is there nothing you can do to change this vow?'

'There may be one way,' she nodded. 'You must find the sun-god and persuade him to release me from this promise. If he agrees to this, then he must remove the scar from your face as a sign that he will give me to you.'

145

So Scar-face left the riverbank, his heart full of sadness and despair. How could he ever persuade the sun-god to give up such a beautiful woman as this? Yet he knew that he must go on this journey, for it was his only hope of ever marrying the girl.

For many moons he travelled across the plains and the forests in search of the home of the sun-god. He crossed great rivers and lakes and climbed the highest mountains, but it seemed that he could never find the golden gates to the sun-god's lodge. He asked many creatures on the way. The wild animals of the forest and the plains were friendly enough, but none seemed to know the way to the sun.

He eventually met a wolverine who had been there once himself, he said. The wolverine offered to show Scar-face part of the way at least. Together they travelled for many miles, until they came to a huge area of water that was both too deep and too wide to cross without a boat. Scar-face was deeply unhappy as the wolverine shrugged his shoulders and said good-bye. 'This is as far as I can go,' he said. 'I do not cross water without a boat, and there is no craft.'

Scar-face was ready to turn back, then, just as he felt the warmth of the summer sun shine down on his back, two white swans appeared in the shimmering lake. They beckoned him to sit on one of their backs. He jumped on the nearest swan, threw his bow and spear on the other and together the swans glided across the great lake to the furthest side.

Back on land, Scar-face travelled for some time in the direction suggested by the swans until he came across a bow and arrow lying above a steep escarpment. He wondered who owned these beautiful arrows but decided not to move them. As he walked further and further into the rocky terrain, he met a youth sieving sand between his fingers. 'You haven't seen my bow and arrows have you?'

Scar-face told him where they were, and the youth decided he would befriend Scar-face. 'Where are you heading?' he asked as they walked along.

'I am trying to find the sun-god. I've been told that he lives not far from here.'

'I am the son of the sun-god,' said the boy. 'My name is Apsirahts and I am the Morning Star. Come with me, and I shall take you to my noble lord.'

So Morning Star and Scar-face set off across the rocky hills until they clambered up on to a bare cliff top. Scar-face held his breath as he looked across at the golden light that shone from the sun-god's lodge. It was the most beautiful lodge that Scar-face had ever seen, decorated with dazzling colours and unusual art. Kokomis, the mother of Morning

Star, waited at the entrance to welcome him in. She was the moon-goddess.

Then the sun-god himself appeared, a most extraordinary power exuding from his golden light. He, too, welcomed Scar-face warmly and suggested he stay and be their guest and hunt with his son for as long as he wanted. But he warned them not to go near the Great Water as there were fierce wild birds who would kill Morning Star.

So Scar-face stayed with the sun-god for many moons, knowing that one day he must ask the question about the chief's daughter. But the time never seemed to be right, for he must be sure that when he did ask, his request would be granted.

Then one day Morning Star ran off into the forest as they were hunting together. Intuitively Scar-face knew he had gone down to the Great Water to kill the savage birds. Scar-face ran after him, and just in time saved the boy from the terrible bird monsters. The sun-god was so grateful to Scar-face for rescuing Morning Star that he asked him if there was anything he could do, any request that he might be able to grant.

So Scar-face told him why he had come to the sun-lodge and about his love for the chief's daughter, and explained how she could not marry him while she was under the power of the sun-god himself.

The sun-god nodded. 'You have saved my son, so how can I not grant you this request? Go back to the woman you love and marry her, and as a sign that I have granted this to be so, I now make your face whole again.'

The sun-god raised his golden hand and instantly the scar disappeared from the Indian's face. The sun and moon gave Scar-face many beautiful clothes and ornaments to take back to the earth world. With his disfigurement gone, his arrival back at the encampment was greeted with awe and suspicion, for no one could recognize this richly dressed Indian, whose face was as radiant and shining as the sun itself. The chief's daughter could hardly believe her eyes, but when she saw the scar vanished from his face she hugged him to her and within a few days they were married.

Scar-face became known as Smooth-face, and together he and the chief's daughter built a medicine lodge in honour of the sun-god in the sky.

Reflections

There is little time for tales of romance and love in the myths of the Algonquian peoples, for their lives were harsh and their close affinity to the power of the forces of nature became the basic ingredients of their myth-telling. Yet this simple and gentle story conveys two different ideas. The sun and moon played important roles in most tribal oral traditions. They were the most notable aspects of the world of gods and supernatural beings, apart from animals that were shape-shifter or trickster spirits. We can see clearly in this short myth how the sun's powerful solar force is already at work, for the girl with whom Scar-face falls in love is already bound to this powerful dynamic energy. She is his sun-maiden and must do his work accordingly. It is for Scar-face to find the sun and plead that she be allowed to marry him. If he returns without his scar, this will prove he has met with the sun and received his blessing.

Animals and nature are the essence of native American people's mythology. Animals are often guardian spirits, and appear in familiar guises throughout North America as givers of advice, setters of tests and general pointers of the way forward. Scar-face meets a wolverine and two swans, which guide him towards the sun-god's lodge. These animal spirits were often able to change shape and form and to move freely from one world to the other, thus their importance and power in any myth symbolizes the ability to transcend the earthly form in which they appear as true guardians of the other world.

From a psychological perspective, Scar-face is armed with an informed consciousness. To one of the ex-suitor warriors, he says: 'I may have a blemish across my face, but not in my heart.' His task is now to find the sun-god so that the girl will be released from her pledge and he will return without his disfigurement. But what does this scar really mean? In its simplest analogy the scar is a physical wound, a reminder of his great bravery as a hunter. Yet in love it does him no favours. He must prove himself in other ways, not just as a skilled hunter, a brave and heroic warrior, but also as a human being who can commit himself truly to love.

The sun-god and moon-goddess are gentle, kindly figures, and eventually rewarding. Their son, the Morning Star, is saved by Scar-face from the savage birds and must be repaid for his bravery. Scar-face's courage is finally rewarded, not with battle-scar reminders, but with the removal of the blemish to show that he can marry the chief's daughter. The test of his commitment has been proved, and he can return 'smooth-faced' and trustworthy in love as he is in courage. The Algonquian family and social cultural background perhaps wisely tested more than just the mettle of a suitable husband for a chief's daughter.

Scar-face's return, smooth-faced and honoured by the sun's blessing, is at last his true redemption. In honour of the sun the couple build a medicine lodge as a powerful reminder of the connection between the natural world, the gods and supernatural beings of the other spiritual world.

Sigurd and Brynhild

Origins and Traditions

THE Nordic gods and warriors were famed for their spirited fighting and their acceptance of death on the battlefield, and the tales are overshadowed by the doom of Ragnarok, which would mark the end and the re-birth of the universe. Whatever it was that drove them fearlessly on, the heroes of the Nordic myths sought lasting fame through deeds of great courage that would allow them to prove their worth. They had little time for self-questioning or psychological awareness, for death was accepted as part of life. To stop and reflect upon their motives was far removed from the instinctual nature required to live in the harsh conditions of northern climes and the needs of survival.

This epic tale of betrayal and vengeance has been treated by artists, writers and musicians over the centuries with both passion and awe. The following version is the basic myth as told in the Norse *Volsunga Saga*. Richard Wagner was inspired to write his music-drama *The Ring of the Nibelung* by a later Germanic version of the myth, and he also took elements from the *Volsunga Saga*. He filled the shell of a great myth with a level of consciousness that incorporates both psychological drama and deeper threads of meaning.

The tale of the cursed ring and the tragedy of the two lovers, Sigurd and Brynhild, stems from the heroic actions of Sigurd's father, Sigmund, which is why Sigmund's story has been included as a preface to provide a framework against which the drama unfolds.

The Myth

SIGMUND was the son of Volsung, and his twin sister was the beautiful Signý. She had been betrothed to the king of the Goths, Siggeir, a man whom she did not want to marry, but she had little choice in the matter. At their wedding feast Odin saw through the corrupt Siggeir. He stuck a magical sword into the heart of the Branstock, a huge oak tree that grew right up through the middle of Volsung's hall, and told the wedding guests that whoever could remove the sword from the tree would become the greatest hero ever known.

Siggeir tried to remove it first but could not shift it even an inch. Volsung himself did no better. Sigmund's nine other brothers tried, but none could remove it. Sigmund was the last to try, and the sword instantly slipped out of the tree as if it had been standing in honey, not solid oak. Sigmund was now declared a hero, much to the anger of Siggeir, who tried to take the sword from Sigmund by means of a bribe, but Sigmund, as any hero would, refused to part with the sword.

King Siggeir eventually plotted to kill all of Sigmund's family. Sigmund's nine brothers were murdered, and Sigmund escaped only because of Signý's quick-thinking. The ten brothers had been bound to the trees in the forest, and each night a wolf would come and devour one of them, until only Sigmund was left. Signý smeared Sigmund's face with honey, and the wolf licked his face instead of biting his flesh. Sigmund caught the wolf's tongue in his teeth and was able to tear out the insides of its mouth and escape. But he had already lost his magic sword.

Signý was determined to bear a great son, but the two male offspring she produced with Siggeir turned out to be weaklings. Signý quite astutely realized that it was probably Siggeir's fault, as he wasn't exactly of warrior status, more a conniving, scheming wimp. She decided to have Sigmund's son and changed her shape by magic. She seduced Sigmund and slept with him for three nights and days continuously, before disappearing. The resulting child was Sinfiotl, and Signý said he was Siggeir's son so that no harm befell the child.

When Sigmund met Sinfiotl they became great friends, and they rampaged around the countryside, killing terrible monsters and evil people. On one of their many adventures they came across two men fast asleep. The men had left a pair of wolf-skins hanging on the wall of their hall, and Sigmund and Sinfiotl tried on the skins to amuse themselves, but their amusement turned to tragedy when they found themselves transformed into werewolves, running through the forests and eating anyone who got in their way. The two werewolves turned on one another, and Sigmund, in his werewolf form, killed his own son, Sinfiotl. Sigmund then saw two weasels fighting, and when one killed the other, it placed an oak leaf on the breast of the dead weasel, miraculously restoring it to life. So Sigmund did this to his dead son, and Sinfiotl was restored to the land of the living. They threw off the wolf skins and decided never to take on animal form again.

While they were trying to avenge the terrible Siggeir, both heroes were captured. Signý found Sigmund's lost magic sword, and, freeing themselves, they set the great hall on fire so that none could escape. Sigmund wanted Signý to come with them, but she remained in the burning palace, sacrificing herself as a penance for her incestuous adultery.

Sigmund eventually married the princess Hiordis, and they had a son called Sigurd. But Sigmund preferred battles to child-raising, and when the time came for him to leave the world and go to Valhalla, Odin destroyed the magic sword by smashing it to pieces. Hiordis picked up all the fragments and gave them to the smith, Regin. She also gave Regin the care of her son Sigurd.

Sigurd was brought up by the astute and wise Regin, who taught him music, the carving of runes, the forging of metal and many other skills needed by a warrior and hero. When he was old enough, Sigurd was given the opportunity of choosing his own horse, and he acquired the great horse Grani, a descendant of Odin's own horse Sleipnir.

One day Regin told Sigurd about a hoard of treasure that contained the riches of the universe, including a magical ring. Unfortunately, unknown to everyone (including Regin), the ring had been cursed by its creator, Andvari, with the power to destroy anyone who owned it.

'Listen well, my son, for this treasure was once owned by a dwarf called Andvari. Among the treasure is a golden ring that the dwarf himself crafted.'

'Why is it so special?' asked Sigurd.

'Because whoever owns this ring will carry its power, for the golden ring has the power to create more and more gold for all eternity!'

'This sounds like a ring of such magic that many must want to lay claim to it,' suggested Sigurd.

'Yes indeed, and for me that is the only thing in life that I desire.'

'Where is it now?' asked Sigurd.

'A long time ago the treasure was stolen by Loki and given to my father. Fafnir, my brother, is also a magician and he turned himself into a dragon to guard the golden hoard.'

Regin turned slyly to Sigurd and smiled. 'Would you be willing to fight the great dragon with me, and recover the treasure so that we might share it?'

Sigurd was a noble warrior and, like his father, ready to set off on any quest or heroic deed. There was no question of his refusing. 'I shall surely come with you to slay the dragon and you shall have your treasure hoard.'

So Regin re-forged the magical sword, using the fragments that Hiordis had collected from Sigmund's sword. Together they set off for Fafnir's lair. The dragon had just eaten and was gorged with food and could hardly move. Sigurd hid beneath a bush beside the stream where the dragon always came to drink, then he took the magic sword, stabbed Fafnir from below and ripped his belly apart.

'Ah, my son, that is splendid! Splendid! You have made me the happiest man in this kingdom. Come! We must celebrate before we share out the treasure. Let us eat the dragon's heart, and surely we shall be honoured!'

So Sigurd removed the dragon's heart. He found a long sharp branch and pierced the heart, then hung it like a spit over the fire. But while the heart was cooking, some of the blood dripped on to his fingers. Sigurd licked the drips of blood from his fingertips and found he suddenly had the power to understand the language of birds and animals. All around him he listened to the voices of the birds, and gradually, as he attuned his mind to their language, he released he was in deep danger. The twittering birds were telling him that Regin intended to kill him and take the treasure for himself.

Sigurd turned just in time to see the mighty sword of Regin thrust towards him. With the speed of a wolf, Sigurd threw his short knife into Regin's chest, then lunged forward, plunging his sword deep into the treacherous man's heart. Sigurd could only gaze on the dead man in disbelief. He had not come for the treasure but to share in the deed of destroying the dragon, and now he had been betrayed by the one man he had trusted. He bathed in the dragon's blood, for the birds had told him it would make him invulnerable, but as he bathed a leaf fluttered down on to his shoulder and stuck to his skin, leaving one tiny spot where the blood had not touched him. The roasting heart was now well cooked, and Sigurd took the meat and ate ravenously, knowing he must journey on to find more adventure, to journey into the unknown.

There was nothing he wanted from the treasure hoard. Gold was not his purpose and he did not wish to take anything, but then he saw one gold ring that glinted and sparkled beneath the dragon's bloated corpse, and he bent down to pick it up as a single reminder of Regin's treachery and proof that he had indeed slayed the great Fafnir. But Sigurd did not realize that the ring he had chosen was the one cursed by the dwarf Andvari.

Crossing Bifrost, the rainbow bridge, he found on a hilltop a palace surrounded by a ring of fire. Inside the palace was Brynhild, a Valkyrie, who had been banished to earth by Odin because she had refused to have sex with him. He had punished her by placing her in a ring of fire where she would sleep forever until a hero came who would be courageous enough to cross the fire and wake her, but Odin had also made sure that her love for this hero would destroy them both.

Sigurd's horse leapt easily across the ring of fire – the fierce stallion had never once refused a jump nor feared anything that Sigurd had dared to do. He tied the panting steed to an iron post, finding the silence, the stillness more alarming than the fire itself. Here was a strange, magical place. Surely, he thought, this palace was filled with some mystery, some encounter or quest. Sigurd crept quietly through the palace gates, certain that he was about to discover a new adventure. When he saw Brynhild sleeping, her golden hair falling over her pillow, her skin softer than any he had ever seen, he must have fallen in love with her. She instantly awoke and, seeing the young and beautiful Sigurd before her, smiled. 'You have come to take me away from here?' she asked.

'I do not know why I have come, but I leapt across the fire that encircles this lonely place and found you.'

'My name is Brynhild. I have been banished to this earth by Odin, and he will allow me to leave here only if someone such as you rescues me.'

For some time they talked, as if entranced by each other's company. Together they walked upon the palace ramparts, watching the fire that burned fiercely around the hill. The skies were icy blue, colder now that the summer was nearly ended, and the palace gardens held only frosty petals of some mountain herbs. Brynhild gave Sigurd fine mead from the cellars, and they sat upon the great stone hearth of the feasting hall, wrapped in cloaks of fur as the sun set low and the skies became golden, yet never dark.

'Gladly would I save you, and gladly would I take you with me, for I am sure that I have fallen in love with you, Brynhild.'

Sigurd had no fear of the ring of fire

'Then take me, my lord Sigurd, for I must confess that my own feelings are similar to yours.'

But Sigurd shook his head. 'I cannot take you away from here yet. I still have a journey to complete, a quest to follow. But I shall return for you, sweet Brynhild, you are my only love and will only ever be my love.'

'I shall wait for you, Sigurd. I have waited this long asleep, now I shall wait with hope and happiness at the thought of your return.'

Sigurd kissed her tenderly the night before his departure, then gave her the stolen ring as a sign of their betrothal and undying love. Later they sealed their love in physical embrace. Then, as the dawn rose, Sigurd stole away from her chamber, unable to face a parting he knew would be filled with sorrow.

As he travelled across the cold, frozen lands, now turning ever chiller as winter drew closer, his fame as a dragon-slayer spread across the kingdom. He knew not what it was he sought, but he journeyed on, believing he would one day discover the mystery and return to Brynhild. She was all he thought about – her beauty, her love, her warm arms and her embrace.

Arriving at the hall of King Guiki, in the land of the Nibelungs, Sigurd seemed a most dashing and highly desirable suitor for Queen Grimhild's daughter. Princess Gudrun fell in love with Sigurd, and his kindness and great deeds inspired all those who met him. The queen heard rumours that Sigurd had already pledged his love to another, but she determined that he should marry her daughter. She bewitched Sigurd with a magic potion, and he instantly forgot his love for Brynhild. He was under such a powerful spell that he was now compelled to marry Gudrun.

Yet Queen Grimhild was still not satisfied. She began to hear rumours about how Sigurd had found Brynhild alone in her palace and had pledged his troth to her. If Brynhild also loved Sigurd with such intensity, it might be possible for her to break the spell that the queen had cast over Sigurd. In her grim determination, the queen brewed another magic potion, this time for her innocent young son, Gunnar. That night she called him to her chamber and secretly poured the magic brew into his wine. She watched him sip the liquid, knowing that his heart would turn to whatever thoughts she placed in his head.

'Gunnar, my son. There is a beautiful woman who waits to be woken from a terrible spell that Odin has placed upon her. But she may only marry the man who can cross the ring of fire that surrounds her. You must go to her and save her, for she is fated to be yours.'

As Gunnar in his trance-like state gazed at his mother, he began to feel a great desire for this woman he had never seen. The spell was working and the queen knew now that if Gunnar married Brynhild himself, she could feed Brynhild with lies about Sigurd, and their love would be forever destroyed.

Full of desire for a woman he had never seen, Gunnar set off to capture the heart of Brynhild. He was no hero, but he felt sure that he could cross the ring of fire. But Gunnar failed miserably, and in his torment he called on Sigurd to help him. Sigurd was still also spellbound by the queen and had no idea who this woman, Brynhild, was. But he agreed to disguise himself as Gunnar and, crossing the ring of fire for the second time, he unknowingly betrayed his own love for Brynhild.

Disguised as Gunnar, Sigurd spent several nights with Brynhild declaring his love for her. But Brynhild could not forget her only love, Sigurd, and was now confused about who she should marry. But Sigurd/Gunnar insisted that he had ridden through the flames and reminded her that it was her destiny to marry any man who did so. She had sworn to Odin a sacred oath that whoever rescued her and dared to wake her she would marry. Sadly, Brynhild remembered this oath. Sigurd had now been gone so long that she had resigned herself to being abandoned. After all, wasn't this man Gunnar here now to take her away from her loneliness?

Sigurd/Gunnar offered her his ring and asked for one from Brynhild to show that she would marry him. Reluctantly Brynhild exchanged rings, giving Sigurd/Gunnar the cursed ring of Andvari. The very same ring that Sigurd had already given her as a pledge of his love.

The real Gunnar changed places with Sigurd during the journey back to Guiki's court and married Brynhild, who, it seems, hardly noticed the difference between the two men such was her sadness at losing her true love. Sigurd set off back to the palace alone, while the happy Gunnar and the miserable Brynhild journeyed together.

On his solitary return and still under the queen's powerful spell, Sigurd came to her chamber.

'So, what news, dear Sigurd? Has Gunnar captured the heart of this Brynhild?'

'Yes indeed. But in my disguise as Gunnar, the lady gave me this ring. Perhaps I should give it to Gunnar, for it is to him that she meant to give it.'

'No, no! You must keep it for yourself, Sigurd, as a reward for the help you have given us. I am sure that Gunnar would want you to have it. Besides, he has no need of Brynhild's ring once he is married to her.'

Slowly, not knowing why, Sigurd fell into a deep despair. Gudrun, the woman he had been forced to marry, was ugly, dark and menacing. He had no time for her company, and yet something in his heart kept trying to tell him there was another, there was one he truly loved. In a moment of great carelessness he gave the ring to the smug Gudrun, knowing at least she would spend time gloating over the golden jewel rather than over him, who could not even bear to touch her.

On the arrival of the wedded couple, Brynhild saw with horror that her true love Sigurd was already married to Gudrun. Worse still, the ring Sigurd had given Brynhild in their love tryst was now firmly placed on Gudrun's finger. As Brynhild lay wretchedly in her chamber, the queen knew there was only one more twist to place in her heart. Brynhild must believe that she had been totally betrayed by Sigurd.

The queen sent for Gudrun. 'Losing your husband to another's love may come to you one day, Gudrun, unless you follow my warning. Listen with care and you shall keep him.' Gudrun's only care was for herself, and the powerful whispers of her mother were eagerly absorbed in the stillness of that cold, wicked night.

The following morning Gudrun visited Brynhild in her chamber. 'You must know the truth about Sigurd, my lady.'

'I wish to hear no more, for I see the ring he gave me now upon your finger. How can this be? I am so wretched with love for Sigurd, but he is your husband. He lied to me, and he has betrayed our love.'

'Indeed, he did it for my sake, sweet lady. He loves me more than life itself, and knowing that you were still waiting for him he took on the cloak of Gunnar so that you might marry Gunnar, and not cast false hopes for his love any more.'

'I cannot believe this! Sigurd promised he would return for me, not return to marry me to another! This is hopeless, he has deceived me beyond all question. Go from my chamber, dear Gudrun. His love for you must be true, for the ring that he gave me, he has given to you. That is the pledge of love.'

'Shall I stay awhile to comfort you?' said Gudrun, but only cruelty sang in her heart, not comfort.

'No. Please go. I must bear the torment that I suffer alone, for you are the sole reason for his madness.'

Fraught with jealousy, Brynhild was convinced that Sigurd had deceived her on purpose. He had pretended to be Gunnar and taken back the ring so that he could give it to Gudrun! Believing that Sigurd had betrayed her, she turned spitefully against him, and in her anger arranged for her brother-in-law Gottorm to murder her once dearest love, Sigurd.

But Sigurd's own memory and his truest thoughts were beginning to return. When he saw Gudrun laughing in the cold night air with the Queen Grimhild, delusions, memories of the past and dreams of Brynhild filled his troubled soul. Somewhere in the past he had loved her, not in his disguise as Gunnar, not in those moments of daring and betrayal, but as himself.

'Brynhild was convinced that Sigurd had deceived her'

L. Vallet

From Gudrun, one evening as she combed her hair, he took back the ring, perhaps remembering now that he loved only Brynhild. But it was too late, for that night he heard strange footsteps on the stone stairs. Before he could reach for his sword, the blackness of death came to him. Another's sword entered his shoulder, just at the place of vulnerability where the leaf had stuck as he bathed in the dragon's blood. As he lay dying, he called for Brynhild, and the golden ring fell from his hand to the stone floor. Brynhild at first was gladdened when she heard the news of Sigurd's death. This was her revenge, this was her betrayal, now rewarded! Yet, as she saw his body lying on the funeral pyre, she was still not released from her love for him. The ring lay in his hand, as if some bird had picked it up and placed it there. A melancholy soul drew portraits of Sigurd's love for her in her heart, and with the sudden realization that Sigurd had never betrayed her, but had been bewitched by the evil desires of Gudrun and her mother, Brynhild threw herself on to Sigurd's funeral pyre and killed herself. The curse of the ring had come true.

Reflections

Sigurd is a Norse hero. He is on a quest, a journey of discovery, similar to the journey we all make through life to find out who we really are and to find a meaning in life. This is something with which every human being is born – a desire to find out who we truly are and what life means to us. Some of us find the key to the doorway through believing in our own gods or our own mythology, others by merely attending to nature. But the hero, as in Sigurd's case, must do it the hard way, through experiencing life and love, and by suffering, which is the way most of us must find a spiritual meaning and psychological understanding in our own lives.

Heroes in Nordic mythology seem to follow the same destiny as those in Greek mythology. Heroes in pre-Hellenic Greece were young men sacrificed to Hera. Although she became best known as Zeus's irrational and jealous wife, Hera and her mother, Rhea, actually predated him. With the rise of the patriarchal gods, both goddesses were assimilated into the Olympian pantheon as Zeus's relatives. Heroes were originally young men offered up to Hera as her martyred husbands-to-be. Similarly, the heroes of the Nordic pantheon sacrifice themselves to a higher calling in much the same way. This sacrifice, however, is at the same time analogous to a search, usually a spiritual search for enlightenment, growth or, as Jung called it, 'individuation'. But whatever path the journey takes, it is also a search for awareness, wisdom and, ultimately, unity with the 'higher self'. Giving up a normal everyday existence, giving up lovers, friends and the comforts of life for a chosen quest is the ultimate sacrifice for any modern-day hero or heroine.

Sigurd's search begins when he slays the dragon. In Western civilization, dragons have usually represented fearsome powers that must be overcome before the hero can continue his quest. In the East, however, dragons are considered highly auspicious, and as such are bringers of fertility and have the power to divert evil spirits. Fafnir, the dragon, represents Sigurd's first test on his journey, a test of the courage that we must all face if we are to make our way through the battles of love and living and, on another level, an encounter with the darker forces of the unconscious.

This first test in overcoming the powers of darkness is complicated by the treachery of Regin, but in the end, it is the challenge from someone whom Sigurd believed to be trustworthy, not seeing the greed and selfishness of Regin's gloating eyes, that is more enlightening for Sigurd than the death of the dragon. Ironically, it is the dragon's blood, rather than the treacherous Regin, that becomes Sigurd's guardian angel. Sigurd loses a caretaker-father but gains personal strength from the betrayal. The dragon's blood also gives him the ability to understand a new language, and it is the birds' twittering that warns him of Regin's designs and reminds him to bathe in the blood he has just tasted so that he will be invulnerable.

So what can this mean for us in our everyday lives? Blood is usually identified with the life-force, the soul, or that which we seek within. Drinking the dragon's blood and bathing in it not only gives a new language, to enable him to connect to his inner world, but also prepares him outwardly to face any conflict or danger. Like Achilles, however, Sigurd has a weak spot – not his heel, but his shoulder. This imagery appears throughout mythology. No mortal hero is totally invulnerable; he is not a god, and precisely because he is a mortal or semi-mortal hero, he must at some point sacrifice himself to something higher than the deeds and the trials. If he is to grow psychologically, he must accept that his human aspiration to seek out who he may become is only human nature.

But knowledge, foresight and intuition can become deeper wisdom only through experience, and so it is that Sigurd must fall in love. Blindly and passionately, believing he is caught up in something bigger, he sees love shining from Brynhild's eyes, a mirror of his own soul.

Sigurd must first cross a ring of fire, but before we follow him on his doomed fate, we must consider the significance of Advari's ring. Rings are common symbols of eternity, of the 'whole', of the completeness and unity of the soul, the spirit and the divine. We give rings as tokens, as pledges, as a way of showing our faith, as Sigurd will do, but the ring he selects from the heap of treasure is cursed with the power to destroy all who own it. One could say that Sigurd has no choice now and that he must surely be destroyed. Yet he had the choice when he took the ring. Sometimes, we take chances, make choices impulsively or make choices with over-cautious and indulgent analysis. It does not matter how or why we make a choice, but once we have followed the path and made the decision, there is no turning back, whether the curse has entered our lives or not.

So Sigurd falls in love, as any human does. He is offered the mystery of this experience to connect more closely to himself, to learn to relate both in the external, other world, and with the inner, darker, unknown one in the realms of self. But like most of us he falls short of his projected ideal. He offers Brynhild his undying love, but cannot take her with him, because the journey of the hero is, by its very nature, unencumbered by commitment. The only commitment he makes to Brynhild is to say he will return one day and as a token of this pledge he gives her the ring.

In order for Sigurd to evolve, to grow, to become aware of who he really is, he must now suffer. Like many stories of human beings striving for what Jung called 'individuation', he must first fall from grace and learn, like everyone else, that pain and crisis are more often our teachers of wisdom than the guru we meet on the road.

The complex and highly involved twist in the tale is common to many later love stories, in which misjudgement, misunderstanding and misery abound. Treachery appears in the form of the queen and her wicked daughter, and a magic potion envelops Sigurd in a trance-like state so that he betrays Brynhild. On one level, the magic potion symbolizes how other people's opinions and venomous words can turn us against our true values, for the potion makes Sigurd lose his memory. How often have you heard someone obsessed with their own power, saying, 'Forget the past, it doesn't mean anything to you now! I am what matters, think of the future. Think of us, of me'? The magic potion dissolves our hearts just as these words do, and Sigurd is suddenly blinded to his love for Brynhild, just as we can be blinded by the light in someone else's eyes.

Grimhild twists Brynhild's love for Sigurd as easily as she mixes the magic potion. This is a woman of Machiavellian cunning, a woman with the skill to poison another's mind. She is an archetypal force that cannot be matched, and her deceit and treachery are replicated by her equally false daughter, Gudrun. This is the shadow side of us all, whether male or female. We can all selfishly, although often unconsciously, manipulate others for our own egotistic devices. It is also the queen, Grimhild, who must conspire to send Sigurd on his final test.

And so Sigurd finally remembers the truth. Stirred by Gudrun's sneers, her body and face now becoming 'ugly' to him, he awakens from his spell, as if something has risen from his unconscious to remind him of the past. His death is inevitable, such is the way of heroes, but symbolically it also represents his transformation. Like Tristan and Iseult, the lovers can be reunited only in death. When it is removed from its literal context, death is a symbol of profound change, as in the tarot card Death, which represents not the end but the cycle of transformation, the death of the old and the birth of the new. The ego at last is able to sacrifice its blinkered old perception to allow in the new and to permit conscious awareness to take place.

For Brynhild and Sigurd only 'death' allows them to escape from the illusion of the physical world.

Pomona and Vertumnus

Origins and Traditions

ROMAN mythology is largely an assimilation of all the myths and beliefs from the peoples that were ruled from Rome. At its height, the Roman Empire stretched across Europe, northern Africa and the Middle East, and it was from this diverse blend of cultures that Roman mythology developed. Before the rise of the empire, Italy had its own pastoral gods, nymphs and a spirit world. These early gods – Mars, for example, was originally the Italian god of farming – became woven into the fabric of Roman myth, as did the powerful Greek Olympian pantheon, whose system became integrated and recycled in Roman culture, thus giving the Romans easy access to an historical and dynastic line that reached back to the earliest gods.

The well-known Roman gods are found in myths that parallel those of the Greek gods. Neptune, Saturn and Jupiter, for example, are Poseidon, Kronos and Zeus. Many of the Greek gods were untamable and unacceptable to the great empire, especially such cultish and pagan gods as Dionysus, who was altogether too disturbing to the Roman mind. Eventually Dionysus re-emerged as the gentler god, Bacchus. This transformation from a wild, unpredictable and passionate divine force into a subtler, more structured and tamable godliness was representative of the merging of Greek and Roman myths that took place in the second century BCE.

The myth below is truly Roman in the sense that it includes earlier Italian pastoral gods, who became assimilated into the Roman mythology. In Roman mythology heroes were not permitted to stay with the woman they loved and could do only what heroes do – follow the call of duty. Thus most Roman myth treats women and the value of love and compassion as secondary to the courageous heroic deeds of the ancestors of the gods. Most Roman mythology may be patriarchal in the extreme, but this myth, based as it is on an early Italian tale, reflects the simple pastoral life before the rise of the Roman Empire. This version, retold from Ovid's *Metamorphoses*, includes the wonderful device of telling a tale within a tale, an added twist to the heady dimensions of unrequited love.

Pomona was the Roman goddess of fruit trees and as such was worshipped widely. She not only had a sacred grove, called the Pomonal, on the road from Rome to Ostia, but she also had priestesses to serve her. Pomona was often associated with Ops, the Roman goddess of fertility, who was thought to live under the earth. Thus her invocation involved touching and handling soil.

The Myth

POMONA lived among the orchards on the Palatine Hill beside the River Tiber. She had been admired by many gods, tree-spirits and satyrs, yet none had ever caught her eye nor turned her head for long. Yet there had been one who had attempted to court her on many occasions. This was the older Silvanus, the god of the fields, but he was too slow and frail, and besides, the trees and fruit she tended were more important than any god who came wooing.

Each spring she would make sure the trees were kept free of blight, that insects were removed from every nurtured bud and that the leaves unfurled without disease. Hers was a thankless task, but it ensured that the summer fruit would ripen well and the apples would swell red and golden in the autumn sun. She worked well, and her life was among the trees, for what need had she of others when nature was her truest friend?

But there was one who shyly followed her as autumn came. He was Vertumnus, the god of the seasons and of the autumn leaves. He was young and beautiful, but he would hide behind the trees when other gods would bow before her. He would climb into the branches of the fruit trees when Pomona plucked the apples for harvest, not daring to speak nor disturb her, but only ever to watch. His was a torment of desire but also of fear, for so many times had he wanted to tell her of his love for her but each time he would hold back, hesitant and inhibited.

Vertumnus turned the leaves from green to gold, from yellow to brown. He would let them fall gently to earth when the breeze blew and rustled the boughs, and as they were ready to leave their boughs he would paint them with a magical palette of ochres and russets, shades and hues of such delight that all who watched the leaves fall wondered at his artistry. Yet his autumnal art was soon over, and, exhausted by the extent of his canvas, he would retreat to the trees where none could see him, awaiting spring so that he could see the fair Pomona again in her garden of apple trees.

So, he spent the summer idly while Pomona busied herself caring for her fruits. Then one day she came quite close to him as he sat among the trees. He saw the beauty of her eyes, the golden shimmer of the sun on her hair, softly falling to her waist, and the way she smiled at her fruiting boughs. Oh, if that smile could be for him! A bee buzzed past her face and she turned to watch it bump and blunder through the higher branches. It came close to where he crouched and as she saw him up there, she turned her head, inquisitive at first, then glancing around, unsure of who he was. But Vertumnus could not bear to face her, his self-consciousness turning his face red with shame. He leapt down from the tree and ran back into the woodland, where he would be safe from his own cowardliness.

But being struck with love is a force that none can deny, and for Vertumnus there was only one thing left to do. He must ask advice from one whom he knew cared. How was he to pluck up courage to even speak to Pomona, let alone tell her that he loved her?

Pales was the goddess of pastures, and she lived among her meadows on the Palatine Hill. She was fair, older than he and had wise counsel. 'Vertumnus, there is only one thing you can do. Listen, if you can change the leaves from green to gold, and from yellow to brown in autumn, perhaps you can change yourself from shy to bold? You are the artist of the leaves, you paint them with your magical colours, why not paint yourself with boldness, so that Pomona may see you in a new light?'

Vertumnus was pleased at her words, yet he was not sure how he was to colour himself with boldness. Should he change his face or change his clothes? In his desperation, he decided that Pales had meant only that he should disguise himself so that he might pretend to be another. In a

'This time he found Pomona among the trees, testing her fruit'

166

different guise, he would change his diffidence and coyness to courage and assertion.

So Vertumnus transformed himself into a merchant, a farmer, a ploughman and a warrior, yet none was successful. Pomona would not even speak with these suitors, let alone allow them to woo her. Whatever change he made, whatever role he cloaked himself with, he could not win her love. In a moment of hopelessness he finally chose to be an old crone. He dressed himself in shabby robes and threw a cloak of torn threads across his head and around his shoulders.

This time he found Pomona among the trees, testing her fruit. It was nearly autumn, nearly time for Vertumnus to work his own magic again. The fruit was almost ripe and Pomona bit into a piece of golden apple and tasted the fruit between her lips. On the other side of the orchard she saw an old woman sitting upon a stone bench. The apple was ripe; perhaps she should share it with the woman, who looked hungry and dejected.

Pomona sat beside the old, sad woman, who offered her a cup of water. Pomona took it gladly. 'Why, thank you, old woman. Here, take a bite of this apple. It is one of the best that I have ever tended.'

Vertumnus shook his head, terrified that she would discover his secret if she saw his face. 'No, you must keep it for yourself, my child. But may I tell you a story while I sit here and rest?'

'Yes, please do. I must rest also, for the days will be busy soon, now that the fruit trees are drooping under their weight.'

'Have you heard the tale of Iphis?' Vertumnus asked, as she drank from his cup again.

'No. Is it sad?'

'Very sad,' he whispered in a low voice. 'Iphis was a poor peasant boy who fell in love with a princess from Cyprus. She was called Anaxarete. No matter how much he courted her and told her how greatly he loved her, she would have nothing to do with him, because he was of humble birth. She hardened her heart so much that it became like stone, so that she would not be hurt by his anguish and pain, nor have any feelings for him. In his great unhappiness he hanged himself, and when Anaxarete found his body, her stone heart transformed the whole of her body into stone too, and she became a statue in the garden where he had died. Don't you think that is a very sad tale?'

'Indeed it is. I would not like to be that princess.'

Vertumnus stood up; these were not the words he had expected. He had truly believed her to be saddened by the death of Iphis, not that of the unfeeling princess! Now he was desolate. There was no chance now that the beautiful Pomona would ever love such a shy youth as he, especially if she had no compassion for the plight of Iphis. Quickly he hurried away across the glade without a word and shook off his torn cloak. Pomona called after him, but he ran faster until the disguise of the old woman fell from him like the leaves from his trees. As he ran blindly through the sunlit glades he turned back into the youthful and handsome Vertumnus. Pomona now saw him as he truly was, shy, gentle and as beautiful as she, and her heart yearned for him.

She ran after him, and as he reached the safety of the deep woodland she called, 'Vertumnus, don't run from me! I did not know it was you who came. I did not know you cared for me!'

Vertumnus turned, uncertain. As Pomona saw him as he really was, she was transfixed with love for him, and he for her. Together they joined hands and kissed as if they had always been meant to be together. From that moment they were inseparable, and their love became part of the cycle of the seasons, as Pomona worked on the fertility of the fruits and Vertumnus cared for the seasons and the cycle of falling leaves. Theirs was a love of perfect union and an eternal passion.

Reflections

This is a superb example of a myth that incorporates early Italian pastoral deities with another Greek-Roman story as its ironic counterpoint.

The simple tale also suggests that being true to yourself makes it possible for another to recognize and connect their own desire to you. Vertumnus is shy, sensitive and withdrawn. He has low self-esteem and believes no one will ever be able to love him. Yet the more he indulges in his over-cautious nature, the more he is rejected. How often do we choose to avoid rejection rather than experience the possibility of a new romance? We hide rather than disclose, we shrug our shoulders and tell ourselves that maybe we are not good enough for X or even, perhaps, that X is not really good enough for us.

But Vertumnus is smitten and cannot escape from the fixation of his feelings and his passion. Pomona appears cold and indifferent, but that is only his perception of her behaviour. Vertumnus himself is aloof, detached and withdrawn, simply because he is so vulnerable. Sometimes we have to change our perception of the world in order to get to know ourselves and to relate to others. So Vertumnus attempts to do just this. He goes to the wise Pales. Some sources suggest that Pales is a male deity or, possibly, an hermaphrodite, but in the myth Pales represents the wise old crone, who, ironically, Vertumnus pretends to be as his last resort as a disguise. Pales's wisdom comes with the words that he must 'change himself from shy to bold', but for Vertumnus this means only one thing. He is not sufficiently self-aware to see the truth behind these words, which is that he should simply be himself and that he should take a chance and boldly admit his shyness to Pomona. Vertumnus can only see this from the point of view of his own, terribly vulnerable perception, which leads him to believe that he must literally transform himself into an image of boldness – that is, a warrior, a person of rank or worth, anything, in fact, that is not him. Yet none of these identities works; no matter whose identity he assumes, it has no effect on the lovely Pomona.

The inclusion of the myth of Iphis and Anaxerete gives us an opportunity to compare the complexities of actually possessing a hard heart with believing that everyone else possesses one. Anaxarete vows not to involve herself with Iphis. He is not of her class, and she fears she might have feelings for him. Ovid's version of this story (which is the one included here) suggests that retribution for Iphis's death comes about because Anaxerete's cold feelings turn in on herself, so she becomes a stone statue. Other versions, however, suggest that Aphrodite turns Anaxerete to stone as punishment for her cruel rejection and indifference. There is still a statue in Salamis, on the island of Cyprus, recording this divine intervention, and a similar story is told by Liberalis about a couple called Arisone and Arceophon. It is perhaps interesting to note that, like the treatment of the passionate and ecstatic rituals of Dionysus, the cruelty of a woman such as Anaxerete and her possible punishment by Aphrodite are here woven into a gentler pastoral myth of bliss, thereby allowing the violent, rather tragic motifs to be assimilated into the Roman ideal of love.

Meanwhile, Vertumnus appears to misinterpret Pomona's reply – or does he? Is it possible that Pomona really does sympathize with the tragic Anaxarete rather than with the sad fate of Iphis? Does she see the truth behind cold indifference, of building boundaries and defences in the psychology of Anaxerete? Is it that Pomona realizes that when someone's heart is turned to stone it is not only the defensive reaction of someone who is just as vulnerably aware as Vertumnus but also the signature of someone who piles stones around their heart because, unconsciously, they cannot handle their own feelings, their own passions, their own needs? Pomona recognizes this state as both reflective of one such as Vertumnus and, equally significantly, of herself.

If Vertumnus had stopped then, not turned and fled away, he might never have displayed his true character to Pomona. He might have sat forever as an old woman, a ploughman, a beekeeper – anything but himself. However, disgusted by the possibility that Pomona empathizes with the cold-hearted Anaxerete, he is forced to show how he truly feels. He has tried to play the part of a woman, to get close to the heart of another woman, for he, like many men, does not understand the heart or soul of women. Yet every man has a female principle within, and the balance of the two energies that make up our psyches, our being-ness, yin and yang, light and dark, female and male, have to be acknowledged within us before we can truly know what it is to love.

For love is about the 'whole', it is about 'oneness' and the acceptance of another human being as both male and female, whatever their gender or sexual preference. Without the male principle there would be no female; without the female principle there would be no male. So Vertumnus shakes off the pretence of womanhood and finds his own female side comes to him, if you like, in the form of Pomona. His projection reflects back at him, and she, his *anima*, his yin energy, merges with him in physical union and eternal bliss. This is the essence of falling in love. To the Romans this myth carries the ideal of man and woman's eternal love. Pomona and Vertumnus were inseparable for ever after: the fruit trees continue to be nurtured by Pomona's fertile nature, while the leaves are cleared by Vertumnus in preparation for winter and the return of another spring. The cycle of rebirth.

However much we idealize love, we know that romantic love may not always last. Like many of the other tragic myths in this collection our projections may fade away or we find it so impossible to live without them we seek another to mirror us again. Yet the very mystery of love is that numinous moment of falling into it. It is unforgettable, magical and, above all, a momentarily and wonderful chance to return to 'self'. Without this mystery we may well have relationships filled with *agape*, *philia* and good, simple human companionship and friendship. We may enjoy the freedom of unconditional love and the ability to love from afar, without demands or desires. But without desire we also lose touch with our souls, we lose touch with passion and with the deep stirrings of a timeless spirit. For what is desire but the very starless realms of our unconscious, where the gods and goddesses lie sleeping within us, ready to awaken us to that moment when we catch a glimpse of ourselves in someone else's eyes, and we are in love.

Further Reading

Apuleius, *The Golden Ass* (trans. Robert Graves), Penguin Books, Harmondsworth, Middlesex, 1950

Baring, Anne, and Cashford, Jules, *The Myth of the Goddess*, Viking Books, 1991

Bédier, Charles Joseph, *The Romance of Tristan* (trans. Hilaire Belloc and Paul Rosenfeld), Pantheon, New York, 1945

Bell, Robert E., *Women of Classical Mythology: A Biographical Dictionary*, Oxford University Press, Oxford, 1991

Béroul, *The Romance of Tristan* (trans. Alan S. Fedrick), Penguin Books, Harmondsworth, Middlesex, 1970

Bullfinch, Thomas, *The Golden Age of Myth and Legend*, George Harrap & Co., London, 1917

Byock, Jesse L. (trans.), *The Saga of the Volsungs: The Norse Epic of Sigurd the Dragon Slayer*, University of California Press, Berkeley, 1990

Campbell, Joseph, *Myths to Live By*, Viking Press, New York, 1972

Christie, Anthony, *Chinese Mythology*, Hamlyn, London, 1983

Davidson, H.R. Ellis, *Scandinavian Mythology*, Hamlyn, London, 1969 (reprinted 1982)

Graves, Robert, *The Greek Myths* (2 vols.), Penguin Books, Harmondsworth, Middlesex, 1955

Hadland Davis, F., *Myths and Legends of Japan*, George Harrap & Co., London, 1913

Hesiod, *Theogony* (trans. M.L. West), Oxford University Press, Oxford, 1988

Hesiod, *Works and Days* (trans. M.L. West), Oxford University Press, Oxford, 1988

Hillman, James, *Revisioning Psychology*, Harper & Row, New York, 1977

Johnson, Robert A., *We: Understanding the Psychology of Romantic Love*, Harper & Row, New York, 1983; reprinted as *Psychology of Romantic Love*, Arkana, Harmondsworth, Middlesex, 1987

Lang, Jean, *Myths from Around the World*, Bracken, London, 1996

Larousse Encyclopedia of Mythology, Hamlyn Books, London, 1959

Mariott, Alice, and Rachlin, C.K., *American Indian Mythology*, Mentor, New York, 1968

Neumann, Erich, *Amor and Psyche*, Pantheon Books, New York, 1956

Nivedita, Sister, and Coomaraswamy, Ananda K., *Hindus and Buddhists – Myths and Legends*, Senate, London, 1994

Osborn, Harold, *South American Mythology*, Bedrick, New York, 1986

Reed, A.W., *Aboriginal Myths*, Reed Books, New South Wales, 1992

Rolleston, T.W., *Myths and Legends of the Celtic Race*, George Harrap & Co., London, 1917

Rosenberg, Donna, *World Mythology*, NTC Publishing Group, Illinois, 1986

Rundle Clark, R.T., *Myth and Symbol in Ancient Egypt*, Thames & Hudson, London, 1959 (reprinted 1978)

Walker, Barbara, *The Woman's Encyclopedia of Myths and Secrets*, Harper Collins, New York, 1983

Picture Acknowledgments

AKG London/Erich Lessing 7; Hamlyn Group Picture Library 95; Mary Evans/Arthur Rackham Collection 19, 167; Mary Evans Picture Library 27, 59 (Innes Fripp), 155 (L. Vallet); Hulton Getty Picture Collection 12, 107, 111.

173

Index